Own Your Brand

An Executive Coach Helps You Refine
Your Personal Brand on LinkedIn®

David Billstrom

Col du Granon Press

Copyright © 2017 by David Billstrom. All rights reserved.

I support copyright. Copyright fuels creativity, encourages diverse voices, promotes free speech, and creates a vibrant culture. Thank you for buying an authorized edition of this book and for complying with copyright laws by not reproducing, scanning, or distributing any part of this in any form without permission. By doing so, you are supporting writers, including me, and allowing me to continue to publish books for everyone.

FlashingRedLight is a trademark of Flashing Red Light, LLC. LinkedIn is a registered trademark of LinkedIn Corporation. Other marks are the property of their respective holders.

Cover Design: Diane Frisbee
Book Design: Karrie Ross, Leandra Ganko, Bethany Donovan
Editors: Sharon Purvis, Elizabeth Lohman

ISBN 978-0-9981384-0-4
ISBN 978-0-9981384-1-1 eBook Edition

Col du Granon Press

For more information about the publisher, visit
ColDuGranon.com.

NOTE FROM THE AUTHOR

MOST OF THE SITUATIONS DESCRIBED in this book are taken directly from my work with clients in my executive coaching practice; however, their identities are obscured to protect their privacy.

When examples include screenshots of the LinkedIn® professional networking service, these are real and are used with permission of the individual shown, in accordance with the LinkedIn Corporation's policy (as of the original publication of this book). In a few cases where images on LinkedIn pages are strangers to me, their photos have been obscured to protect their privacy, also in accordance with LinkedIn Corporation's policy. Throughout the book I use "the LinkedIn service" as a shorter form of the LinkedIn professional networking service.

I have no direct relationship with the LinkedIn Corporation, other than as an early and loyal customer. It is my intent to provide an unbiased and pragmatic guide to using the LinkedIn service.

DEDICATION

FOR MY PARENTS, WHO TAUGHT all five of their children from a young age that they could accomplish whatever they set out to do.

TABLE OF CONTENTS

PREFACE

I've learned from decades in business that companies don't do business with companies; people in companies do business with other people. I was a slow learner, but eventually I grasped the simple truth that *relationship* is the foundation of any kind of success, in and out of the business world.

You probably already knew this.

The capability of the Internet to bind together people from around the world has accelerated with the broad acceptance of social media—at this writing nearly 2 billion people use Facebook and nearly 500 million use the LinkedIn service. Hundreds of millions use Pinterest, Instagram, and Twitter. It is nearly impossible not to be included in social media. Even if you have tried to avoid it—your friends, family, associates are posting about you.

You probably already knew this too.

Who could miss the role social media has come to play across the world and in your daily routine?

And yet.

I'll bet you're not paying attention to the effect social media has on your job, your professional life, and your business relationships.

Why would I make that bet? Because the majority of the people I meet in business either neglect their online reputation, or outright ignore it. Some sound downright guilty and regretful that they're not up to date, while others are nearly haughty about how they're above all of that "Facebook nonsense" and "I hate social media." Some claim that they're "old school" and prefer to rely on existing relationships.

I get it. I was in denial myself for many years.

And then I realized everything is different. For me, it was a conference call.

I'm sure you realize that the conference call is a staple of the business world (and increasingly a tool used for non-profit boards, volunteer groups, and in continuing education requirements for many professions). And I'm sure you realize that it is also typical for most participants in such calls to have their computer in front of them, so that they can see a presentation that is the subject of the call.

Several years ago, I was on such a conference call with a handful of people. As we were getting started, one of the participants asked me about my prior work at another company—he said "I see here you worked at Disney at the same time I did. Did you know so-and-so?"

I was speechless. He obviously had my LinkedIn Profile called up on his computer, and was checking me out while the meeting got started. He was nonchalant and casual about it.

Then it dawned on me that this wasn't the first time he had done this, and a few moments later I realized that others could do it too. And would. That's when I was jerked out of my denial. Everything had changed.

Today, it is the norm. You are still in denial if you don't think people on the other side of the table aren't checking out your online presence before, during, or after a meeting. Every meeting.

As of this writing, approximately 65% of adults (18–65) in the U.S. are members of the LinkedIn® service (and more every minute). We are living in a world where everyone can see you, whether you want them to or not.

The insight that *everyone can see you* is as fundamental as the insight that people do business with people, not companies.

It has forever changed how we relate to others and how we get things done: conversations, sales, clients, vendors, partnerships, hiring, being hired, and media coverage. There is no part of the practice of business and professional life that hasn't changed because of the availability of online information about you.

And it isn't just business. You will see the effect at church, in non-profits, while volunteering in the community, and in politics, both elected and appointed positions.

Professional and business relationships have been forever changed by this new norm. It will not be rolled back, but will in fact go deeper and wider.

This book is about embracing this new norm of offering yourself as an online presence, not avoiding it.

And more: this book is about recognizing the *opportunity* of your online presence. Where you can offer both your reputation and your preferences, even your passions, for the work you are doing and the work you would like to do. What you've done, what you can do, and what you want—the essence of your personal brand.

Despite my original denial, I have even come to *love* this new dimension of relationship in business.

I have seen over and over that a thoughtful and careful presentation of yourself online makes everything better: better meetings, better interviews, better choice of candidates, and even helps developing great customers (and great vendors).

Interactions with others, particularly early in relationship, are more efficient, effective, and grounded when you offer a personal brand. The possibilities multiply when your brand is authentic and purposeful, distinct and unique, and easily and conveniently accessed by others.

In short, when you really *own your brand*, everything you do is more effective and efficient.

And how did I get here?

I've helped dozens of clients hone their brand, as part of the assistance I provide as their *executive coach* or *entrepreneur coach*. Almost every client I've worked with in the last few years has needed to define, or at least refine, their brand. Doing this over and over revealed the need for a pragmatic, step-by-step method that anyone could follow.

I've been coaching entrepreneurs and executives for more than 20 years, starting when I was first invited to join the board of directors for a technology company back in 1996.

Helping business leaders in the work of leading has been a passion of mine ever since. Ten years ago I made it my business.

Today I work with no more than 15 clients at a time, some with early startups, others with roaring successes, and a few who are executives in large, public companies.

My own career has included small companies and startups, as well as public corporations such as Disney and Intel, and seven years as a venture capitalist. I've worked for stock options in small companies, and I've been an executive in large companies. I've served as CEO and president, and also as the "Interim CEO" a few times. I've also emptied the wastebaskets and worked on projects for customers as just one member of a larger team.

I estimate that I've attended approximately 700 board meetings (so far) and I've hired (and fired) executives more times than I can count. I've worked to recruit key employees, company leaders, and board members. And I've raised money from angel investors, venture capitalists, and strategic investors, as well as doing the challenging work of selling companies to acquirers. At current count, I've worked with more than 45 companies as an investor, co-founder, board member, or advisor.

All along my path, I've endeavored to understand the person on the other side of the table. I've learned that you can't raise money, you can't recruit great people, you can't get a great job for yourself, and you can't sell products and services unless you have a *relationship* with the other party.

So when I realized that the ubiquitous and persistent access to information about people wasn't a problem, but an opportunity—I formalized the methodology that I had used with my clients. This book teaches you that method.

To inspire better relationships and more effective engagement, I want you to be able to tell others *who* you are, what you *want,* and *why* you want it. I want you to *own* the impression you make on other people—not just the people you know, but the people you haven't met yet. I want you to have a thoughtful brand, and make it visible to everyone online.

I want you to stop hiding what makes you great.

Own Your Brand

*An Executive Coach Helps You Refine
Your Personal Brand on LinkedIn*

INTRODUCTION

You have to be careful who you meet.
You can't unmeet them.
~ Jodi Lynn Anderson

I AM AN EXECUTIVE AND entrepreneur coach. I help clients achieve their goals by supporting them in their work with strategy, tactics, and introductions to other people who can help. I first did this 20 years ago as a member of the board of directors of a young technology company, and then offered the same kind of help to founders when I ran a venture capital fund, and eventually coaching work became my day job.

I am energized most when helping my clients face challenges encountered in business and life, and I love helping them surmount these challenges to achieve their goals.

While there are many aspects to a typical coaching engagement, over the decades I have seen two characteristics in almost every client: first, they are not crystal clear about what they want. Second, even if they are clear about what they want, they could do a far better job of communicating to others what that is—and why they can do it, have done it, and should have it.

This book helps you with those two challenges. I will help you clarify what you want and describe more effectively and persuasively to others what you want and who you are. This is your *personal brand.*

Think of your brand as a sturdy stool relying on three legs in a tripod: what you do, what you've done, and what you want to do. I'm going to take you through the process of defining your brand, and we'll explore the many reasons why you want a crisply-defined brand.

In this book you will find out why your paper resume *isn't* your brand. And even if you have a website, that's not your personal brand either. **Part 1: Your Brand** lays out why you need a brand, and the difference between a LinkedIn Profile and a resume (and why that matters).

You are about to leverage the free LinkedIn service to promote your brand, and keep your network informed. **Part 2: What LinkedIn Can Do For You** discusses and reviews the common pitfalls (and hidden advantages) of the LinkedIn service. The service is excellent and free, but I'm going to help you use it in a "selfish" way. A way that serves you best.

In **Part 3: The Method** we'll follow a step-by-step methodology to uncover what is important to you, and what you're truly about. We'll gather evidence for everything you've done in life up to now, and use that evidence to help establish credibility that you are who you say you are—and that you can do what you say you can do!

This is where we define the three sturdy legs of your brand: what you do, what you've done, and what you want to do.

The outcome from this method will become your LinkedIn Profile, but you will find that it also works for your website, your bio, and anywhere you need to present yourself.

With the hard work done, in **Part 4: Loading LinkedIn** we'll cover the "mechanical" process of loading your text into the LinkedIn service. We will cover every detail of setting up your brand. You may be surprised to learn in this part of the book that certain fields of your LinkedIn Profile are *best left blank*. I'll tell you which ones, and more importantly, why.

In **Part 5: Launching LinkedIn** we're coming down the home-stretch, with a few guidelines and hints for "going live" with your new and improved personal brand hosted on the LinkedIn service.

Part 6: Care and Feeding of Your Brand covers the all important requirements for keeping your brand current and credible, so it will remain relevant (and effective). We'll also discuss the specifics of how to accept invitations to connect on LinkedIn, and how to make invitations to connect. We'll discuss how to continue building credibility for your brand online.

In finally in **Part 7: Results** we'll wrap up your efforts and we'll talk about why all this matters, why it was worth the work you did to hone your brand and tell the world what you really want. I'll provide you with a few examples of successful personal brands.

Spoiler alert: I maintain a Hall of Fame for excellent personal brands on my website; perhaps *your* profile will qualify?

You may be wondering if this method is for you. Most people assume LinkedIn is something you turn to when you want a new job, and that a personal brand is something that only famous people or highly-visible leaders need to worry about. I don't subscribe to that view. I think each of us already has a personal brand, often called our *reputation.*

It isn't a question of whether you need a personal brand; the question should be "is my reputation accurate?" or "does my reputation enhance or obstruct my efforts building relationships?"

Entrepreneurs are constantly meeting new people, forming relationships and trying to convert others to their cause. I warn founders of startups that they will need to succeed at roughly 50 to 100 relationships in their first year. Some are obvious: investors, customers, and key employees. Others are less obvious: the landlord, a good attorney (or two), an accountant, vendors and suppliers, contractors and consultants. Entrepreneurs want the best, and the best of each of these people are choosey and discerning.

The entrepreneur's personal brand is not only their calling card, but a kind of catalyst that can make all those relationships more effective and efficient.

And entrepreneurs aren't just found in Silicon Valley startups. "Entrepreneurs" also run small businesses, family businesses, and even large corporations. "Entrepreneurs" also organize and lead non-profit organizations, clubs and churches. They run for office, and are appointed to important volunteer roles in their communities. They raise money, lead schools, and some of the bravest entrepreneurs work for change from

3

within government agencies large and small. Citizens that take action for causes they care about are also a kind of entrepreneur.

Basically, if you care about something and want to effect change or make progress, you will succeed in part because of *your reputation*. Your reputation will precede you in anything you do, and honing your personal brand so that it is accurate, credible, and authentic will make you more successful in everything you do.

And finally there is one other kind of reader I want to reach: the incredibly competent people I've met in my travels, successful in their respective jobs. Happy and satisfied, they're among the best at what they do. They're happy where they are and with what they're doing; they aren't looking for a job, and they prefer a low profile—I'm sure you recognize this kind of person.

And yet. I want them to offer their personal brand to the world even though they *don't* need to. Their competence and accomplishments are too often a secret—until we read their obituary. Too often, few know what they've done and what they could do. I think they too should present themselves thoughtfully and deliberately, putting their excellent work in the view of others. At a minimum, their brand will inspire others.

And who knows what engagement may ensue for them? Perhaps they're just the right person, the missing puzzle piece needed to complete a team pursuing a worthy cause. We *all* need to do a better job of presenting ourselves to the world.

Read on to find out why, and how.

PART 1:
Your Brand

Build a good name. Keep your name clean.
Don't make compromises, don't worry about
making a bunch of money or being successful.
Be concerned about doing good work. Protect
your work and if you build a good name, even-
tually that name will be its own currency.
~ Patti Smith

YOU WILL LIKELY HAVE MORE than one career, and certainly a number of jobs. Perhaps you already have.

If it isn't already evident to you, you should know that experts have documented that people are living longer—much longer. Life expectancy for today's U.S.-born 7-year-old is 89 years. We are living so much longer that pension funds (and Social Security) will be inadequate to fund those longer lives. And at the same time, the concept of life-long employment is already long gone, even in government.

In other words, people of both middle age and those just entering the work force can expect to hold multiple jobs throughout their lifetimes. Many can contemplate multiple careers, sometimes completely different than their original career or profession. Which means that they'll be hired not only for what they can do, but also for who they genuinely are *as a person*.

Your reputation will largely determine the opportunities you enjoy for the rest of your life.

And not just in the workplace, but in clubs, volunteer opportunities, local politics, nonprofit organizations, and even in your church.

Doing what you want, with the people you want, is about forming relationships and engagement. Whether you are approached, or you approach someone else. And relationship is developed, in part by how you present yourself.

Your Reputation

A powerful force is at work today that wasn't an issue when I first entered the work force at 15 years old in 1976. Only the U.S. Social Security Administration knows about my first W-2 job, because I didn't make enough money to file taxes and was still living at home with my parents. And there is no other regulatory compliance that dates back to that time, so no one knows I worked part-time in a convalescence nursing home as an orderly.

No one knows I had that job—and no one, including me, can prove that I had that job—although you can see income for that year on my lifetime social security statement. I could have been the best employee or I could have been terminated for cause. My performance in that job long ago is essentially secret.

This lack of accountability was true for many of us until the 1990s. In part due to regulatory reporting requirements, but primarily because of the ubiquitous and pervasive nature of online data, social media tools on the Internet, and our Internet-connected culture… today, no one can escape their reputation. Everyone you know, everyone who works with you, and everyone who works for you… knows of your reputation.

Think about that for a moment. This means that every mistake, every aspect of your professional reputation (and often, your personal reputation) is knowable, at some level and in some way.

Not only is this true, but it cannot be avoided (except perhaps by extreme measures, such as not working at all and not attending school, which obviously isn't a possibility for most of us).

I often remind my clients in coaching sessions: you can't un-know someone; you will know that individual for the rest of your life, and they'll know you. Now, how do you want to handle yourself in that meeting tomorrow?

If you can accept this insight and get past the creepy feeling that you are exposed, then you can embrace this as *an opportunity*. An opportunity unprecedented in the history of work: you can actively edit and publish your reputation.

But it isn't just damage control. What about your accomplishments, the unique aspects of you that make you yourself? What about your passions? Your brand can tell *that* story.

Curate Your Reputation

I regularly counsel my clients not only to make their reputation visible, but to *curate* their reputation. By this I do not mean a simplistic "only show the good side" of their professional face, but to present their authentic self.

And to provide proof. Provide corroborating evidence by virtue of their life experience, their self-awareness of strengths, and their formal certifications and awards.

Curating your reputation, particularly with a focus on authenticity, will help you be much *more efficient* in your engagement with others.

What does that mean?

Efficient results for my clients have included new and unsolicited inquiries from customers, potential employers, partners, and even vendors that they didn't know they wanted to meet—but did.

An efficient personal brand has also triggered inquiries from nonprofits and other organizations seeking their unique talents for a position on their board of directors, an invitation to serve as an adviser, or a volunteer role that was a "perfect fit."

Many of these incoming inquiries are more appropriate, more focused than ever before... because the reputation presented by my clients is more accurate and more focused than ever before!

In other words, if you present yourself accurately and if you include *what you like...* then you have improved the chances that a potential customer or potential employer will select you out of the crowd, because they will be *drawn to like-minded people.*

There is literally no downside to curating your brand, and the opportunities for engagement that result can be truly unique. Why not?

One Example

One of my clients illustrates the value of a personal brand in a clear way. He is an architect with a portfolio of work and excellent references. He held a position with a medium-sized firm for more than a decade, then operated his own practice for a while before joining a new small firm. He could have done all of that without a brand.

However, as we worked together to define his brand, I discovered quite by accident that he has a passion for airplanes and holds a private pilot's license. There was no mention of this in his resume or his LinkedIn online resume, and he doesn't participate on social media such as Facebook. In the first pass through his personal brand, he left it out because it has nothing to do with architecture or employment history. It was essentially a secret.

As I urged him to rediscover every aspect of himself and what makes him authentic, he mentioned the passion for flying. I urged him to include this in his personal brand, and also to include the narrative of how he came to discover this passion (a captivating story, involving the cockpit of a Boeing 747). He stopped hiding what makes him great.

Today he specializes in architecture for aviation, and he loves it. His personal brand is part of why he does that work, and it assures that he'll do more of it in the future. By revealing his authentic self in his engagement with business partners, he didn't just get the architecture work he enjoys, he got the architecture work with aviation *that he loves.* And he is likely to get more of it.

What are your passions? Are they part of your brand? Do you have a brand?

But What About My Resume?

Your resume is not your brand. A paper resume or curriculum vitae ("C.V.") still has a place in certain professions or jobs where the culture of the profession requires one, as it describes specifically and precisely what you've done.

For example, if you are teaching or doing research in academia, such as in a university or national laboratory, it is expected that you will have a formal and precisely-worded C.V. Business people may not realize that the academic's C.V. typically runs at least 25 pages; some are much longer. Obviously such a lengthy and detailed document is not a brand (although it could contribute to one).

There are other jobs and careers that require a resume, and job recruiters will request one as the very first step in the application process in many large companies (although some now require a LinkedIn Profile instead).

As you know, a typical resume documents each position you have held, along with educational achievements and metrics such as awards and certifications. But the resume is not a brand, because the resume fails to provide a broader picture of the individual outside the workplace and almost never explains why the individual did what they did at work.

With the traditional resume, it is usually left to the interview process to "uncover" and "discover" the motive, passion, and commitment behind each accomplishment.

Why wait? Why put friction into that process? Consider the advantages of inspiring the reader by illuminating your motives and passion for your work *right up front*. Don't make them work for it!

Accomplishments are fine, a key dimension of each individual. But they aren't enough. If you've ever been the interviewer, you already know this. As you interview, you're seeking to understand the other party, in particular their motivation.

And as an interviewer, you are probably aware that you are in jeopardy if you ask questions that could be construed as bias, as thoughtful regulations prohibit questions about age and marital status. There is literally no legal way for the interviewer to determine if the candidate is willing to talk about these and other topics, which is unfortunate if the candidate is willing to talk about "personal" information, passions, and experience.

The resume will not have this information, and the interviewer can't ask—but the candidate can offer this information as part of their brand. Hobbies, family life, passions, really anything can be included to present the "whole person" as a context for the professional accomplishments. Present your authentic self, as transparently as possible.

Yes, you may well need to maintain an "old school" type resume or CV for your particular profession, but it isn't your personal brand. For that, we need to do some detective work. We need to "connect the dots" of your life experience, to explain not only what you've done, but why you did it. And above all, to speak distinctly and clearly about what you want to do next.

We need all of that to be obvious, without the need for an interview to *pry it out of you.*

Delighted With What I am Doing

I know a number of people who truly love what they do and enjoy the people they work with every day. Awesome. They may not know how blessed they are (although the ones I know seem to be very aware of how lucky they are).

And it may go on for many years. Or not.

The reality of life is that it is dynamic, and ever changing. That dream job in that great location, may evaporate tomorrow. And such change could be the best thing that ever happened to you.

We all know fine people who have made the choice to stay exactly where they were born and raised. And we know others who moved away to the "big city" or foreign country that was in their dreams.

And then the situation changed—for oh, so many reasons. Family, career, love. I've been there myself.

In 2008, I couldn't find North Carolina on a map without help, and suddenly by 2010 I lived there (of course, it wasn't quite that simple). Midwest-born, raised in California, college and career in Pacific Northwest and the Silicon Valley… and all of the sudden I live in the South. It's no movie, but it definitely wasn't in the script that I originally imagined.

My point is that you may be delighted with what you are doing, well-paid, respected, and established. And then it's time for change, sometimes when you least expect it. In my case, the move to the South was part of the best change that I've ever been blessed with in life: a loving partner, great colleagues, fascinating geography, beautiful country, fine music, wonderful friends.

But with that change in geography, how do I connect with others, especially professionally? How do they know who I am? What do I love to do? What do I do well? In other words, *how will they know me?*

I'm Looking For A Job

A thoughtful personal brand will also help you get a job. Not only are you making it easier on the recruiter by presenting your passions and motives explicitly right up front, instead of requiring an initial phone screen interview to get this information… but you will inevitably be seen in a more unique, separate light.

Recruiters face thousands of candidates in the form of resumes, and it can be challenging to stand out and be noticed among all of that noise. A brand with passion, motive, and capabilities made explicit is, by definition, unusual and unique. Yours is more likely to get noticed.

And the more you reveal, the more likely a recruiter is going to see "a fit" that truly is a fit. From your selfish perspective, a specific inquiry from a recruiter is always better than a cattle call of all candidates with certain credentials—which wastes your time if there isn't a fit.

I'm Not Looking For A Job

In a moment, we'll talk more about how your brand helps you outside of the job-seeking mode, such as volunteer work, community service, and other leadership opportunities. But first, I'll share my experience of why you should carefully refine and promote your brand even when you're *not* in job-seeking mode: there are two good reasons for this.

First, I counsel my clients to always be ready to look for work. This isn't paranoia, but simply good common sense.

As we've already discussed, lifetime employment with one company is a disappearing possibility for most of us, even if we really would be happy with it. In my lifetime I have seen the virtual guarantee of employment in both civil service and certain private sector jobs erode away, along with the retirement plan and the pension payout. If you have a job now, it may not be there in a few years. And if you have a job now, your retirement funds may not be there when you retire (and you may not consider Social Security enough). You have at least some chance of needing a different job, sometime in the future.

And then there is the possibility that you will not find the work you truly love, right away. You may need to work your way up to earn the experience, credibility, and contacts required to even get the job you truly love, let alone succeed in that job. Along your path, you may need to pursue and land jobs.

For example, I remember the moment in 1983 when I first realized I wanted to be a venture capitalist and help entrepreneurs succeed (I sat in the audience of a panel discussion by venture capitalists at a small conference in Portland, Oregon). As it turned out, it would be 17 years before I landed that plum job I wanted.

For me, it took landing a new job on five different occasions over the intervening years to get to the one I wanted the most. Each of those jobs helped develop the skills, contacts, and experience that I needed to be a venture capitalist. I was utterly unprepared for venture capital in 1983, and even if I had landed a job, I would not have succeeded in the job. You too may have a dream job in mind, far off now, but worth working towards… requiring you to get a new job or two along the way. Always be ready to look for work as a step in the right direction of your eventual goal.

I tell my clients that the second reason to develop a brand even when you're not looking for a job is because some of the best opportunities come looking for you, rather than when you're looking for them.

As an aside: I often need to counsel my clients to be open to unexpected job inquiries and unusual clients, as they seem all too ready to turn down offers before they even understand them.

It is common for people to turn down offers before they actually receive them. It is best to actually understand the "offer" or opportunity thoroughly, before sending any negative signals to the person making the inquiry. You don't know what you're turning down if you don't know what the offer actually is. And there is no cost to discuss the possibility, and such an interaction builds relationship.

Another story illustrates the point. Because of my lengthy technology industry history, I was approached several years ago to consider interviewing for the CIO (Chief Information Officer) position for a large county in another state. My first instinct was to laugh, since I've never been a CIO and I've never worked as a government executive. But I stifled my amusement and took the call, asking plenty of questions.

As we discussed it, I better understood the inquiry—an "outsider" was attractive, experience with technology transitions was paramount, and a shake-up of the status quo was desired. I realized that I had quite a bit of context for this opportunity, as I had volunteered in county government for over a decade, I had owned or invested in several companies that focused on state and local government customers, and I have a passion for improving our communities. It was a better fit than I would have realized.

I eventually declined the inquiry and the interview since the job would require relocation, and I truly believed there were candidates far more qualified than me.

But as I developed the method in this book to help my clients define their personal brand, I realized that very little in my own LinkedIn

13

Profile would have inspired this inquiry—it was only possible because a long-time colleague knew me, knew my capabilities and passion, and thus knew "my brand" even better than I did.

He inquired precisely *because of my personal brand.* I realized that if I wanted more engagement and more opportunities like this—I needed to make it easier for others to "see me." I would need to improve my LinkedIn Profile so that it would present my personal brand.

And another example: one of the best jobs I never took was an unsolicited, totally out-of-left-field inquiry from a startup company in France in the 1980s. They asked me if I would move to Paris and join their team. Like my clients today, I turned them down before I found out how much it would pay, whether they would move me, and whether they would teach me French. Yes, they did all of that for the American they did hire (a friend of mine) and he thrived.

I sometimes imagine how life would have evolved if I had taken that opportunity more seriously, let alone had moved to Paris.

I think we can agree—we all want inquiries for jobs and gigs that we don't even know to ask for... even if we don't know that they exist. These kinds of opportunities can be the pivotal points in your life.

In fact, the best time to develop and curate your personal brand might be precisely when you are *not looking* for a new job. Without that pressure, ou may be more free to be authentic and consider what you really want.

By the way, that's exactly how I did eventually get that coveted venture capital gig in 2000. It came to me; I didn't go looking for it (another story for another day).

But What About My Website?

Some clients ask if their website is a better vehicle for their brand than LinkedIn. And that's a good question—many professionals who operate their own practice (or work within a larger practice of similar professionals) are compelled to offer a website to explain their services.

Examples of this include law firms, accountants, consultants, advertising agencies, marketing firms, and yes, business coaches. Their websites exist primarily to provide contact information, information about services offered, credibility by virtue of existing (happy) clients, and above all, a presentation of their "brand" (although they might not call it that).

By necessity, each practice or firm is promoting the brand of the practice, the *brand of the firm*. The firm's brand is *not* the same thing as a personal brand.

For example, take a look at the website for the R2C group in Portland, Oregon (r2cgroup.com), a successful marketing agency. Notice that they're highlighting their portfolio of work, the breadth of clients, and the breadth of staff.

They're casting a wide net to haul in the fish that are a good match for the firm. Ideally, they'll pursue many clients but only accept the clients that are the best fit for their agency. Presumably they keep their brand "broad" to get as many possible clients to choose from as they would like, so they're *not* specific about each professional in the firm.

If you are a prospective client of a professional firm, you may skim through the firm's website and like what you see. Your next step is to make contact and find out if they can do the work you need. Experienced clients know that the key is to find out if they *want* to do the work you need. A motivated vendor does a better job than an unmotivated vendor, for obvious reasons.

So suppose you click on more information about R2C at their website, and make your way to the executive creative director and his bio. Happily, the R2C website offers a full page of information on Steve Diamond, but it is mostly a list of his former clients—typical for a professional services agency, especially a marketing agency. By the end of the page I have a glimpse of Steve, but no real details.

This example is about as good as it gets for a professional service firm's website, and information about their staff. R2C does it very well, in fact.

But short of calling up Steve and interviewing him, how do you find out: Who is he? Why is he there? What does he love to work on?

It may feel like you're stalking him when you start digging around, but you're not. In this age, you're "researching" solutions to your problem on the Internet.

This issue of hiring professional services is a frequent frustration for many.

For instance, I have seen my clients struggle to hire a graphic designer who truly "gets" them, can communicate effectively with them, and can deliver work on time. It is not unusual to hear of multiple failed attempts to hire a great provider for their graphics needs. How do they address this issue each time they consider a new vendor?

You might assume an interview is in order, but even that can be a challenge. Not all of those interviews are "efficient" or even accurate. Many firms will send a senior partner or contributor to the first meeting alongside a junior staff person. And that senior talent is a rare sight after that, leaving substantial responsibility for the actual work on the shoulders of the more junior staff person. This might work out just fine (it often does) but again, the client is wondering about the staff person—their abilities, passions, and motives. The firm's website will be silent on this.

So yes, a professional services firm needs a website, and a clear articulation of their brand. But it's not enough.

The professionals in that firm, each one, *need their own brand.* Each of their brands need to effectively communicate who they are, what they have done (as opposed to what their firm has done), what they love to do, and what they want to do next. In other words, the personal brand makes the process of finding the right fit more efficient for both the firm and the potential client.

And in Steve's case, he does. Find him on LinkedIn and check him out. As of this writing, his full profile is available, with one of the best personal brand statements I've seen. I would definitely consider hiring R2C Group, and I'd ask for Steve first because of that profile.

(No, I don't know Steve nor the R2C Group, and they do not know that they are in this book; this is truly a random selection via the Internet.)

Even More Reasons

By this point, you're probably tired of reading about why you need a personal brand. Enough already, eh? Not so fast.... Even if you're happy in your job, you're sure you're employed for life, you're already retired, or you don't have a professional services firm… there are still more good reasons for presenting yourself authentically to others via a personal brand.

Here are a few more scenarios, ripped from the headlines of my coaching practice.

One of my friends is retired and happy, fully engaged in the business of enjoying the next phase of her life. She was inspired to contribute to her community by joining the parks and recreation commission, which is made up of community members. Members of the commission, as in many communities, are appointed by the town's council. Despite the town's small size, not all of the council members know of her and her background. The process doesn't support an interview, as the council votes on the basis of the applications made by the candidate.

This is an excellent example of where her personal brand, available to both the existing commission members and the town council members, could have enabled a positive, informed appointment. And her colleagues on the commission could have welcomed her to the group, aware of her strengths and passions. A more efficient presentation of her authentic self would have made their job of including her in the group more effective. Furthermore, she had gifts in organization and promotion that were not apparent until months after her appointment—more inefficiency.

Another friend of mine wanted to help a nonprofit organization apply for a grant because of his passion for the non-profit's cause. His offer was eagerly accepted by the nonprofit's board of directors, and they went to work on the grant application. It quickly became obvious that very specific letters of recommendation and endorsement would be required for the application, but two of the best candidates for providing such endorsements had never met him. He was essentially a stranger asking for a favor.

Imagine how much more efficient and more effective the solicitation of endorsements would have progressed if my friend had a personal brand—a brand that would have included not only his life experience, but also his passion and commitment for the cause. He could have referred to his LinkedIn Profile when requesting the endorsements, as a way of introducing himself.

In this case the grant application was completed successfully, but the relationship formation necessary could have been far more efficient. The obvious relevance of the volunteer grant writer's passion could have been highlighted, rather than relegated to a minor footnote.

A final example: a talented client of mine sought inclusion in a creative writer's workshop, an illustrious group that does not accept all applicants. He was not accepted. As I began working with him, I could only find a scant profile on LinkedIn, listing two academic job titles (no description or details) in the past, and no reference to his current work in fiction. Google revealed only academic papers to me when I searched on his name. He was essentially invisible and hidden, from the eyes of workshop organizers, who were creative writers themselves.

Yet when other writers meet him and talk to him, their connection is immediate. They recognize him as one of their tribe, and someone worthy of their support and encouragement—this has actually happened since his unsuccessful application. And it illuminates the challenge: we are often evaluated and judged, from afar and via the Internet. In his case, there was little or no relevant information. We've since adjusted that issue by following the method in this book, and now he is no longer invisible. His real, funny, and satirical self is now presented in the light of day for all to see.

He needed a brand, and so do you.

PART 2:
What LinkedIn Can Do For You

If you're an actor, even a successful one,
you're still waiting for the phone to ring.
~ Kevin Bacon

BEFORE WE TALK MORE ABOUT your brand, let's first understand the LinkedIn service. It is a powerful tool, but it *isn't* for networking. And it's *not* for hosting your resume either.

But it *is* an unprecedented and irreplaceable vehicle for your personal brand.

What LinkedIn Isn't

The LinkedIn service as originally framed was a social network for business, a method of "networking" with others. Note that it launched before Facebook existed and that it attempted to provide an online way to "network" (as a verb).

Early promotions indicated that you would use it to get an introduction to a person you didn't know, via a person you already knew—literally, a *connection* (the LinkedIn term). The idea is that you maintain a collection of your connections.

The LinkedIn service enables you to see not only all of your 1*st Degree* connections, but also all of the connections of *your* 1st degree connections have with others—these are your *2nd Degree* connections. The idea is that you can then ask for an introduction to a person separated from you by 2 degrees (or even 3 degrees). As a result, you have access to thousands (or more) of connections.

For instance, I am not directly connected to Reid Hoffman (founder of LinkedIn and a co-founder of Paypal). However, Reid is a friend of Barak Berkowitz, a Silicon Valley startup executive and a long-time colleague of mine.

Barak is one of my *1st Degree* connections, and Reid is one of Barak's *1st Degre* connections, so as a result, Reid is one of my *2nd Degree* connections. Figure 2.1 shows how Barak Berkowitz is our shared connection.

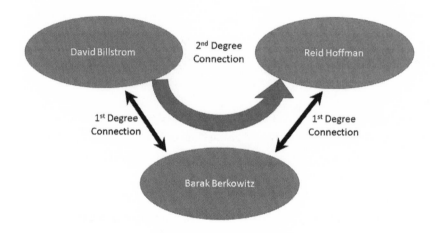

Figure 2.1 1st Degree and 2nd Degree connections.

We should note that each LinkedIn participant can protect the identity of their connections from the general public via their privacy settings. However this effectively cancels one of the core values of the LinkedIn service—so I do not recommend you do this.

A key functionality of the LinkedIn service is that you can search on the name of anyone in the world, and if they are on LinkedIn, you will see their LinkedIn Profile.

You will also be informed of how you are connected to this person. When I search for Reid Hoffman, for example, his profile includes an indication that he is a *2nd Degree* contact to me.

You may also recognize this concept as *the Bacon Number*.

In 1994, the actor Kevin Bacon inspired a parlor game in which movie fans attempt to find the shortest path between any actor and Kevin Bacon. For instance, Kevin Bacon has a *Bacon Number* of 0, and Ed Asner has a *Bacon Number* of 1 (because Asner worked with Bacon on a movie together). Robert Redford has a *Bacon Number* of 2, because he has not (yet) worked on a movie with Bacon, but he did work on a movie with Meryl Streep. Streep and Bacon also worked on a movie together, prior to Streep's work with Redford.

The concept gained national attention when it was featured on an episode of the television show *The Daily Show* in 1996. The concept also led to the development of a popular game, and to Kevin Bacon founding SixDegrees.org in 2007, a charity leveraging the concept.

The LinkedIn *2nd Degree* connection is equivalent to a *Bacon Number* of 2.

I can see from the LinkedIn service that I have a connection to many people in high technology in 2 degrees because I have a number of *1st Degree* connections in the LinkedIn service with a number of the "Kevin Bacons of high technology" such as Barak Berkowitz (who seems to know almost everybody).

This is the embodiment of the "networking" service that LinkedIn promised to provide at their initial launch: a way to reach anyone via intermediary connections.

The basic functionality of "networking" in the LinkedIn service still exists, but like all startups, the company and its services have evolved. And good thing—my first experiences with the LinkedIn service in 2003 were nearly worthless.

Back in the day, I was the 1,621st person to join the LinkedIn service, invited by the previously mentioned Barak Berkowitz. Barak joined the day before I did, on the first day of the official launch of the service. To put this in perspective, as of 2017 there are more than 467 million subscribers.

I created my free account, allowed LinkedIn to see the contacts in my address book (about 2,500 at the time), and learned that a handful (about 12, as I recall) were already on LinkedIn. The service suggested that I "connect" with those 12 that were already members of the service, and I did.

The service also suggested I start inviting my other contacts, to encourage them to join LinkedIn so that I could link to them, as Barak had done with me... using a semi-automatic method. I tried this too.

The response was tepid, at best.

Debi Coleman (a former Apple executive, and an investor in one of my early companies) asked me, "David, why in the world would I join this service? You already have my cell phone number, and you sent this message by email. Why do we need it?"

I explained that this way we could introduce our contacts to each other.... She immediately replied that she would prefer we do that by email.

Frankly, I couldn't disagree. She declined to join LinkedIn.

So I pretty much ignored LinkedIn for a long time—a couple of years, in fact. I would accept requests for connections (more on that in a moment) but I would rarely request them. My life continued to unfold, I continued my career as a venture capitalist, I expanded my work with startups, and I didn't think much about LinkedIn much at all.

What LinkedIn Really Is

Four years later, my venture capital work was winding down and I found myself wanting to reconnect with colleagues across the country (and the world) in search of what might be next for me. I turned to LinkedIn, but frankly spent most of my time in my own contact database, which by then had grown to about 4,000 people (you meet a lot of people in the venture business).

After reaching out to a few, I realized that I needed help with the sheer scale of my contacts. Why? Emails bounced, jobs had changed, and even geographies. It is a reality that today our lives are mobile and dynamic. Only a handful of colleagues and friends use the same email they had in 1993 when I left Intel. I needed help.

I quickly found new value in LinkedIn that was fundamentally not available in my address book, and hard to find even with the advantage of Google Search. What could LinkedIn tell me? *Where my colleagues currently worked.*

I could also see their job title, and if it had been a while, the job they had before the current one... and that job title as well. I quickly realized by looking at their connections that I was reminded of other colleagues (that we both knew), and where they were currently working. It was a gold mine of information!

And LinkedIn could do it "at scale"—I could access the (reasonably) current information on each of 4,000 contacts without any special effort. Brilliant!

That was my cue to re-engage with the LinkedIn service.

IT'S WHO YOU KNOW

Although I rarely "network" with other people using LinkedIn as the communication tool, I do use the *network data* in LinkedIn. As Debi Coleman sagely observed all those years ago, I can send an email directly to the individual 99% of the time and obtain the conversation I want, and that is generally more authentic and effective than using the "connect" request that LinkedIn provides (we'll talk more about when and when *not* to use "connect" in **Part 6** of this book).

I use the *network data* almost every day. With an individual's profile in front of me, a quick scan tells me about the individual's experience, and just as important, a glimpse of *their* network for key indicators.

What am I looking for? Their LinkedIn Profile shows me who we know in common—after all, they might be good buddies with one of my long-time friends. That's happened more than once.

Or they might have connections with someone I don't respect, or even two or three of these...that's useful information (although I suspend judgment until I get to know them better, this is a warning flag that I have learned to heed).

The size and shape of their network indicates not only the kind of people they know, but the geography and industries where their network resides—in other words, the *shape* of their network.

The *size* of their network often indicates how long they've been using this tool, which is one indicator of sophistication in business.

And the size of their network is also an indicator of their engagement with "modern" tools (LinkedIn has been available for 14 years as of this writing). Utilizing the LinkedIn service is no longer a sign of an "early adopter"—and the avoidance of embracing it is another warning flag that the individual may not be sophisticated in business.

As I've written about separately, it is rarely productive to make general requests. In any request, it helps your contact if you can make a *specific* request—something that they can respond to with a specific answer. To do this, you want to be able to quickly review your network and find the people you already know who may be able to help because they work at a certain company, live in a certain geography, know a certain industry.

LinkedIn is an ingenious way to access your network in database form, constantly kept up to date by the residents of the database, instead of by you!

Today I have about 6,500 professional contacts, and it is not physically possible for me to maintain their current contact information. In fact, I struggle to keep track of the core 500–600 contacts. This is a simple problem that we all have.

Even in writing this book, and browsing through my LinkedIn database, I've been surprised with news of colleagues and been inspired to reach out to others. And I barely lifted a finger. Awesome.

This is the first of three properties of the LinkedIn service: it is *your database of professional contacts,* which you access, but do not maintain.

LINKEDIN WILL HOST YOUR PERSONAL BRAND

The second property of the LinkedIn service may not be obvious, as it is hiding in plain sight.

Let me explain. Many users of LinkedIn have posted a version of their old-school, paper resume in their LinkedIn Profile.

Some of these are elaborate and provide every detail; while others keep it so short that you can't tell really what they've done, only where they have worked.

And any kind of resume on LinkedIn is going to interest a recruiter somewhere, so people using LinkedIn in that way have had *some* success with employment inquiries.

Or so I've heard.

None of my colleagues and none of my clients have *ever* had an inquiry that resulted in an actual job offer from the *"my resume is on LinkedIn"* method. I'm not saying it doesn't work; I just don't know of it working.

Yet, as we've already discussed, you are being evaluated via your LinkedIn Profile on the LinkedIn service by other parties all the time. For free. Whether you know it, or not.

If you can free yourself from the notion that you are somehow required to offer your paper resume on LinkedIn, you can use the LinkedIn Profile as a *free host for your personal brand.*

The LinkedIn Profile is currently a deep and wide page for each LinkedIn member, with multiple sections that the member can fill out—or leave blank. While the structure is relatively restrictive, the experience can be shaped by the member to present their personal brand to viewers (whether members or not).

The potential for this free hosting service is hard to exaggerate. Searches for an individual's name on Google, for instance, will reveal a LinkedIn Profile for that individual typically on the first page of results, often in the first 3 or 4 results listed. *After no special effort on your behalf.*

Note that this is available to all searchers with access to Google, not just the 467 million (as of this writing) LinkedIn registered members.

And while the LinkedIn service is structured, we should also note that there are effectively *no controls or approval process* for this hosting service. You alone control what is in, and what is not—how you describe yourself, and what you share about your experience and your passions.

This is the second property of LinkedIn: it is a (free) hosting service for your personal brand, feeding search engines and available to 467 million members. And it is under your control. Hiding in plain sight.

EASY REFERENCE CHECK

You have probably already realized what the third property of the LinkedIn service is: the easy reference check.

One of the earliest features of LinkedIn was the **Recommendations** section, where you can recommend specific contacts in your LinkedIn network for work, and they can recommend you for work. Originally envisioned as the equivalent of the old-school references section of your paper resume, this has become much more powerful in the hands of the skilled user.

Members of LinkedIn browsing your profile will see these recommendations, which are essentially short letters of reference.

And the relevance of their recommendation about you is obvious, as the viewer can click through to learn more *about the person making the reference,* via *their* LinkedIn Profile, thereby magnifying (or diluting) the relevance of their endorsement of you. Handy, eh?

Note that they see not only the recommendations made about you, but also the recommendations *you* make about others. That's an opportunity (and a potential stumble too).

Fortunately, these recommendations are offered in your LinkedIn Profile without any special effort on your part (other than your initial approval of each recommendation by one of your connections). We'll talk more in **Part 6** about how this works. Suffice to say, these are significant.

For the viewer, this provides an easy and effortless method of checking the references on a candidate *before* the interview is conducted.

It simply cannot hurt to have positive and specific letters-of-reference displayed as part of your LinkedIn Profile. These endorsements of your character and ability cannot easily be "unseen"—so they are helpful in making your brand accurate and specific. As are your careful and thoughtful recommendations made for others, another way to "see" you in a professional context.

This is the third property of LinkedIn: it offers reference checks (curated by you) to the reader *before they are needed.*

OTHER USES FOR LINKEDIN

Understandably, the LinkedIn service is constantly striving to offer additional functionality and features. For instance, in a format similar to Facebook, many LinkedIn users make posts to their "wall," which in turn is provided as a feed to other LinkedIn users. The feed allows viewers to "like" and comment on the posts, which encourages engagement between users.

Unlike Facebook, the LinkedIn feed does not tend to be random bits of information, videos of cats and cucumbers, or political statements. When I have time in my day to glance at my LinkedIn feed, I almost always see posts that are relevant to business, capitalism, entrepreneurism, or one of my professional interests.

If you have utilized Facebook as part of your social media strategy in a consumer business, then you can appreciate the possibilities for utilizing LinkedIn as part of a social media strategy in a business-to-business marketing campaign.

Other features include the ability to form and participate in groups, to pay for advertising, to pay for job listings, and to "endorse" users for specific skills.

We'll talk more about how to get the most out of your LinkedIn membership in the **Part 6**, including making posts and keeping your profile current.

But I Already Have A LinkedIn Profile

If you're like most of us, if you already have a LinkedIn Profile, you "created it" by transferring some or all of the information from your paper resume into your online profile. I've been there, I understand.

But if you didn't do that, by all means *do not start making entries into your profile now.* Hold on a second, and finish reading this book.

If you start editing now, you will be missing the opportunity to define your brand. And you might instead studiously enter details into your LinkedIn Profile that (almost) no one cares about.

The rest of this book will show you exactly how to get the most out of your LinkedIn Profile, in a thoughtful and systematic way. There are a few ways to stub your toe on the LinkedIn service, and I'm going to help you avoid this.

Most of the existing LinkedIn Profiles are boring, boring, boring. No one is reading them. No one is learning about the fascinating and awesome people who created them, because the best parts are hidden. What a shame.

LinkedIn Summarized

To sum it all up, we're using the LinkedIn service for your personal brand for 3 reasons:

1. LinkedIn hosts your personal brand in your LinkedIn Profile in a way that is available in detail to members and also visible to everyone on the Internet, world-wide. For free.
2. LinkedIn is your database of professional contacts, which you access but do not maintain.
3. LinkedIn offers reference checks (curated by you) to the reader *before they are needed.*

In **Part 3: The Method**, we'll follow a careful process to create (or refine) your brand, put it into your LinkedIn Profile, and obtain connections and references to boost your credibility.

But before we do any of that, there are **five urgent actions** that you absolutely must take if you *already* have a LinkedIn Profile.

Do This First

Because 467 million members (and the worldwide web) can see your LinkedIn Profile, there are a few urgent actions that I recommend you do first, before anything else. These five actions fall into the category of *primum non nocere* (first, do no harm).

If you have a LinkedIn Profile already, do this:

Action #1 Work in (relative) private—turn off updates
Action #2 Reserve your spot
Action #3 Audit your profile
Action #4 Fix the dumb mistakes
Action #5 Upload the right picture

We're not ready for surgery, this is first aid. Stop the bleeding, keep the patient breathing.

All of this is perhaps two hours of work, at the most. So knock it out now, and then go ahead to the next chapter to start the real work of defining and presenting your authentic self as a brand.

If you don't already have a LinkedIn account, then jump ahead to page 38, to the sidebar *Joining LinkedIn.* You will want to do this to secure your spot before someone else does, and then return to the step-by-step method of developing your personal brand.

Now let's cover the five must-do actions:

Action #1
Work in (relative) Private—Turn Off Updates

By default, certain changes you make to your profile are immediately and automatically "broadcast" to your network. LinkedIn's intention is to help you out, by notifying your network that you have a new job, for instance… when all you meant to do is add a job or change a title.

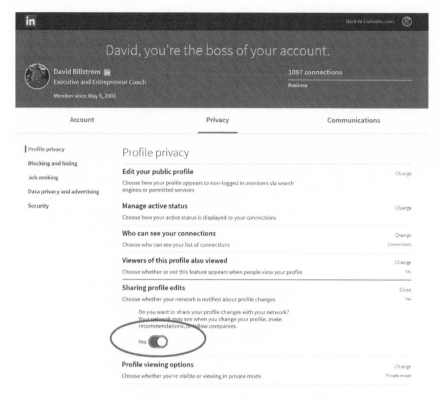

Figure 2.2 Before anything else, turn off notifications!

As you work through the steps in this book, you'll be making a number of changes. The default assumption of the LinkedIn Service is that you would want all of your network to know that you've had a change in status.

But we don't want to make all of the changes in your profile "in public"—not only is that unprofessional, but you run the risk of generating too much activity and fatiguing your audience.

So turn off updates for now (see Figure 2.2). When you've got your profile in top shape, you will turn them back on again…precisely so that your network will be alerted about what's new with you. But until then, you want to work in relative privacy—others can still see what you've done, but they won't be alerted to the change.

Action #2
Reserve Your Spot

In **Part 6** we'll discuss how you will be offering your LinkedIn Profile to everyone you meet, but in this context our concern is that your personal brand is presented in the *best possible light*. Every one of the 467 million profiles on LinkedIn has a unique URL (aka website address). By default, it is something like:

https://www.linkedin.com/pub/david-eliot/102/299/339

A string of gobbly-gook that isn't memorable, or easy to write down accurately.

Yes, it can be clicked when provided as a URL in a PDF, email or website. But we can do far better... for free!

We get to choose a *custom URL,* so that it looks something like this:

https://www.linkedin.com/in/davidbillstrom

I always urge clients to do this immediately, since once you have selected it, it is yours *forever.*

And while there are only a handful of David Billstroms in the world, your name may not be so unique and you will want to define a URL that is easy to remember, easy to spell, and of course, unique.

There is no such thing as a free lunch, but (at least for now) there is a free custom URL waiting for you at LinkedIn that is yours forever. Do not delay.

The following set of screens will show you exactly how to do this (see Figure 2.3 on the next page).

Figure 2.3 Click on the gear icon to access your LinkedIn URL.

View your profile.

Find the "gear" icon *(this may be a different icon in your browser)* next to your URL link just below your picture (see Figure 2.3 above), which will illuminate when you hover the cursor over the URL link.

Click on the icon...You will see a screen like this (see Figure 2.4).

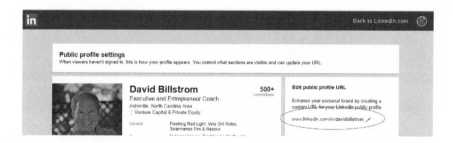

Figure 2.4 Click on the pencil icon to create a custom URL.

Find the **Your Public Profile URL** section in the upper right of the screen (highlighted in Figure 2.4)

Find the pencil icon next to your URL link *(or whatever your browser provides as an icon)* and click on it. Your URL will become something you can edit, in a rectangular window...as you can see here (in Figure 2.5). In this example, you can see my custom URL "davidbillstrom."

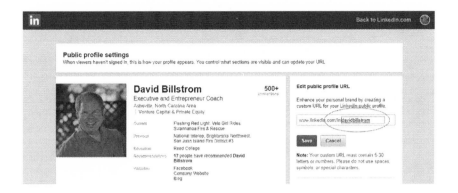

Figure 2.5 Click Save to secure your free, custom URL.

Type in the unique name or handle you want to use (keeping in mind that you cannot use spaces).

Keep it short—you'll be printing it on your business card, if you still use one of these.

Don't make it laborious to type it into a computer or smartphone. Your full name is a good choice. Don't get too cute, and don't make it too specific (e.g., "MarketingDave") since it is permanent, and your brand will evolve over time.

Examples:

reidhoffman
davidbillstrom
petecandler

Click save and you're done! It is yours forever.

Action #3
Audit Your Current Profile

So before we go any farther, open up your LinkedIn account right now, and select View Profile so you see what every visitor will see.

What does a savvy viewer look for at first? Obvious typos or errors in your profile. They will also notice a few more things:

- The URL for your profile (see above, Action #1)
- Number of connections
- Your picture

Make note of these. Consider printing a PDF of your profile that is seen by visitors. We'll use that to keep track of what needs improvement and progress towards making those improvements.

Please *do not* take action to correct your profile text, or your picture. This is your "audit"—take note of the problems, but *don't* start writing new content just yet. I promise you, soon enough we'll get to the specifics of how to improve what you found in your audit.

Action #4
Fix the Dumb Mistakes

That said, there are the obvious problems that need immediate remediation.

Can you imagine a typo on your old-school-style paper resume? I didn't think so. Use the same high standards with your LinkedIn Profile.

One way to check for typos and misspellings is to copy your text and paste it into **Word** (or **Google Docs**) and let the technology highlight potential errors.

For right now, simply go over your existing profile with a close eye and make sure you've spotted and corrected any typos or spelling mistakes. Resist the temptation to start editing your profile, because we've got a better way to do that (unfolding in the rest of this book). Your mission now is to fix only the dumb mistakes.

Action #5
Upload the Right Picture

One of the most valuable features of LinkedIn from the perspective of the user is the photograph of you. This helps them remember you, perhaps where they met you, and sometimes it even reminds them why they like you.

Many of us are far more visual than textual, and while we may forget your name, we won't forget your face.

Research shows that humans are especially good at noting subtle variations in faces and remembering them, so it is *a key part of your brand.* Recent data indicates someone is *14 times more likely* to find you on LinkedIn if you have a photo in your profile.

What photo should you choose?

First, understand that *any* photo is better than no photo. No photo at all says, "I'm so clueless that I only use dial telephones mounted on walls, but if this mobile phone thing is really here to stay, then next year I might get one."

While I completely support the value of minimizing technology in our personal life (and enjoy off-the-grid vacations myself), it is simply naïve to ignore the 467 million members of LinkedIn and the negative effect on your personal brand if you wave a flag and declare that you don't need technology.

Upload a picture so that you meet the minimum standard for LinkedIn sophistication. Introducing a theme that we'll return to again and again in this book: be thoughtful about your presentation, and be authentic. What's the right photo within those guidelines?

The *right* photo to choose is one in which you are:
- Shown in your best light, figuratively and literally
- Dressed for business, whatever that is for your industry
- Looking into the lens (so you are looking at the person looking at you)
- Smiling sincerely

The *worst* photo to choose is one that:
- Shows you indecisive or unsure
- Shows you unhappy or worried
- Is "arty" or "creative"
- Doesn't look directly at the person looking at you (evasive)
- Doesn't show your eyes at all (the same behavior as a criminal about to hold up a liquor store)

Think this is easy to get right? Here, in Figure 2.6, are a few photos of business people I found on the Internet in less than 5 minutes:

Unsure   *Unhappy*   *Seeking Revenge*   *Witness Protection*

Figure 2.6 Typical photos of business people found on the Internet.

It's not clear why these individuals used these images—perhaps to catch our eye (they caught mine) and be differentiated.

But first impressions can't be undone, and I can't imagine a business relationship with any of these individuals.

I will admit that two of them could harbor ambitions as actors in Hollywood, in which case I might change my opinion. But I doubt it.

Even if you are a creative person in a creative field (such as Hollywood), your personal brand is best served by a welcoming, smiling image as someone easy to do business with, someone who is sincere about good relationships. Save the arty/creative look for your portfolio, your website, your body of work, or Facebook.

For your first impression on the world's largest network of business contacts, smile directly at your future business partners, and let them see who you really are.

On the next page (Figure 2.7) are a few positive examples gleaned from the LinkedIn Profiles of several of my clients.

How can I help?   *Meet for coffee?*   *Isn't this great?*   *No problem.*

Figure 2.7 A few of the many right pictures found on LinkedIn.

It will not be a surprise to learn that the best photo for your personal brand is achieved by paying a professional to take your photo (the lingo in the trade is a "headshot").

But if you're on the cheap, then my advice is to browse LinkedIn and choose the photos you like of others (such as the ones above) and mimic their setting. Choose a neutral texture, or at least a background that is not distracting.

Get someone to take a photo with their smartphone while you position your body at an angle from the camera, turn your head to look towards the camera (your head off axis with your body), remember to lift your chin, look directly in the lens (or smartphone) and smile. Really smile.

A hint from the professional who took my headshot: she had my loving wife stand right behind the camera, and told me to look at her. I'm not particularly handsome, but I love looking into my wife's eyes, and the result it is one of the better photos of me.

Take a lesson from call center research: callers can tell if the operator is smiling, and if the smile is sincere. Over the telephone.

Imagine the effect your photo has on viewers online.

Joining LinkedIn

If you don't already have a LinkedIn account, now is a good time in the process to sign up.

The minimum information required to sign up is

- First and last name
- Email address
- Industry
- Zip Code

Use your real name (we'll adjust this later, if necessary), the email address you want to use to correspond *with the LinkedIn service* (it will *not* be exposed to the public unless you want it to), your real zip code, and an Industry that corresponds with the work you like to do now. All of these can be changed later, so do not stress about a careful choice.

As you follow the signup procedure, skip past all of the "helpful questions" until you have the basic profile displayed.

BEFORE YOU DO ANYTHING ELSE...
Re-read the previous section for **Action #1** (work in privacy) and **Action #2** (reserve your spot). You can also upload the "right" picture (**Action #5**) now or leave that for later.

But be sure to *turn off* your network notifications (**Action #1**) and reserve your custom URL (**Action #2**) before progressing farther in this book.

Special Situation: Multiple Profiles

Quite a few of my clients have found to their surprise that they have two profiles on the LinkedIn service, usually because of an early attempt that was aborted or otherwise ignored years earlier. LinkedIn doesn't require unique names, since that isn't realistic with a worldwide community of users, so this is easier to do than you might think.

If you suspect that you might have started the process of creating a LinkedIn Profile on a previous occasion, conduct a *search on your own name* before setting up (or updating) your LinkedIn account. Don't forget alternative spellings of your name, and with and without your middle initial.

If you find two (or more) profiles for yourself, then seek assistance from **LinkedIn Help** for your specific circumstance.

They offer procedures for combining the profiles, or more properly described, combining *accounts* so that you don't lose any connections in the process. This is key. Even if you have just a handful of connections, you don't want to lose them (and your contacts don't want to lose you).

LinkedIn Help anticipates a variety of problems, such as: you have forgotten the password; you've forgotten the email account you used to set up the account in the first place; or you don't know the email account used to set up either account.

Access this help from the drop-down menu in the upper-right with your profile photo.

Pro tip: in general, you will want to keep the account with the most number of connections (in other words, the "larger" account) and move the connections from the "smaller" account into that larger account.

Don't worry about the existing content in your "smaller" account—that is easy to recreate, and you will find that this book is going to challenge your assumptions about what content should be in your profile anyway. That said, you may want to print a PDF of the existing content in the "smaller" account before making the prescribed changes.

Next Up

Okay, the urgent tasks are done. You don't look careless with typos, you can make as many changes as you like without immediately broadcasting them to the world, you have secured your custom URL, and your smiling face can be seen on the Internet. Grab a cup of coffee or tea, and take a moment.

PART 3:
The Method

Oh, give me land,
lots of land under starry skies
Don't fence me in

Let me ride through the wide country
that I love
Don't fence me in
                    ~ Bob Fletcher and Cole Porter

NOW WE ARE GOING TO DEFINE your brand. Or, if you've already put
effort into developing your brand, we'll refine it and optimize it so your
brand is more effective. I've developed a step-by-step method that has
worked with dozens of clients, and you can use it too.

In this phase, you'll write your life experience and work history into
a new format and get it ready to load into the LinkedIn service in **Part
4** (using a specific method).

As previously mentioned, I recommend doing this entire exercise in
Microsoft **Word** (or **Google Docs,** or similar) before using the relatively
limited interface of the LinkedIn service. Get your draft done first. Do
not work in the LinkedIn service.

And yes, this is the hard part.

Defining Yourself

In my work, I rarely encounter people who have a thoughtful and comprehensive view of who they are and what they offer to the world. Perhaps this is because we're all a bit self-conscious about ourselves, or perhaps because we'd all rather have someone else tell us why we're valid and valued. Perhaps it touches the same sensitive spot that we encounter when we talk about our compensation or ask for a raise.

Or perhaps it is because we're afraid to dream of what we really want. Let alone ask for it… and tell others what it is.

Yet this is a key requirement for success.

What do you do well, and what do you enjoy doing? What do you offer a team, a company, an organization, a non-profit, a client?

I want to put special focus on determining not only what you offer, but what you *love* to offer. Your passions, your "dream" assignment.

The first step in curating your brand is to understand who you are and what you offer. We'll do this in a simple process that requires peace and quiet—and a commitment to sticking with it for a few hours.

Step-by-Step Process

We're going to use a six-step process to define your brand:

Step #1 – Discover (or Rediscover) Your Assets
Step #2 – Tell About Each Asset
Step #3 – Draft Your Brand Statement
Step #4 – Build Credibility with Your Life Experience
Step #5 – Revisit and Refine Your Brand Statement
Step #6 – Create an Awesome Headline for your Brand

Let's get started…

Step 1:
Discover (Or Rediscover) Your Assets

Find a quiet place to work, take a fresh piece of paper (I recommend an old-school approach initially, rather than a computer) and make a list of your professional assets.

I mean this in the broadest possible way: assets can be pragmatic skills, accomplishments, certifications, experiences, capabilities… really anything might qualify. Don't get too picky or precise. Your first draft list might look something like this (see Figure 3.1):

- Super organized and rarely late for anything
- Write neatly
- Easily form deep and meaningful relationships with others
- Loyal to friends, family, and employers
- Hard working
- Not much ego
- 25 years of experience in my industry
- Love making order out of chaos, even if someone else's chaos
- Bachelor's degree and some work towards a Master's
- Deep skills in Excel, accounting software, and really any software I've ever found
- Loving towards animals, and loved by animals

Figure 3.1 Example of a first draft Asset List.

We call this list your *Asset List*. And it is the basis of everything else we do in defining your brand, so don't rush it.

ANYTHING GOES

As you can see in this sample Asset List, we're all over the map. This certainly isn't a list of jobs, nor is it purely "skills"—in addition to skills like the use of Excel and organization, we've got examples of attitude, behavior, and preferences…being on-time, loving animals, hard worker, ethical, and even self-assessment of ego. This is a great list (and an actual one from a client).

Some of these Assets have big implications—as a potential employer or professional investor, I would spot "not much ego" and "25 years experience" and "love making order out of chaos" as three very interesting Assets. I have seen these consistently in very successful people. On the other hand, some are probably not significant, such as "write neatly" and "loved by animals."

But we actually *don't know yet which Assets aren't significant.*

What if the future opportunity is directly related to animals, farms, and agriculture?

Or graphic arts, where precision and neatness are paramount?

The point is: you need to start with a holistic list of everything you offer others. If in doubt, put it on the list.

Don't attempt to limit your Assets. Be sure to include everything, not just your "work life" (remember the architect with a pilot's license?).

And who doesn't want to be on a team with someone who "laughs easily?"

Really, include everything.

NOT A BALANCE SHEET

And another thing: we're not looking for a pro/con list, of strengths and weaknesses. We don't want to create a "balance sheet" of assets and liabilities. We just want the strengths. This is your Asset List.

Do not attempt to put in priority. Just get the authentic list of what you bring to a team, a challenge, a client, a family, and your life.

In any order.

WHEN YOU ARE STUCK

Some of my clients find this exercise difficult, and are initially stuck with a form of writer's block when faced with that blank piece of paper. They're not alone.

It's tough to candidly and frankly assess what we've done, who we are, and what we love to do. I sometimes find that clients are fearful of writing down, let alone saying out loud, what they really want and what they really love to do (in fact, that is one of the most common motives for engaging an executive coach).

One technique you can try on your own is simple.

Get out of your own head by considering what a dear friend or long-time colleague would say about you. Imagine them saying, "She's just the person you want when you need..." and see what they say next.

If that comes up blank, then heck, go ask them.

Really, ask them: "What am I good at?" But don't argue with them, just write it down. Seriously, do it.

Step 2:
Tell Us About Your Assets

I often suggest that you give your Asset List a rest at this point. Let some time go by, so you have the opportunity to think it over as you go about your life, go for a walk, go work out.

Then come back and feel free to edit your Asset List, or even add to it as you remember new candidate Assets.

PRIORITIZE

Before I encouraged you *not* to put your Assets in priority, keep the creativity flowing with every idea, crazy or not.

Now I want you to take the step of putting your Asset List in order of priority, with #1 being your strongest Asset. How to prioritize? You can use any method that speaks to you, but I'll urge you to put first the Assets you are *most proud of* developing in your career and/or life.

Another consideration is placing a high priority to Assets that are your *passion* or connected with your passion. For instance, you may be very good at organizing order out of chaos and it is something you truly love to do. So put that Asset high on your list, maybe at the top.

If you have two Assets you consider of equal importance, but you love one more than the other… that's the tie-breaker.

It's okay to be *aspirational.* You may have an Asset that isn't part of your professional life, say riding your bicycle or running in endurance races. But if that is what you truly love to do, it gets a high ranking. This isn't about the eye of the beholder; it is about you trying to *understand your authentic self.*

NARRATIVE

Now select the top 10 (or so) Assets in your prioritized Asset List, and write a *very short story* for each one. At this point you might want to switch from writing on paper to typing into a document on your computer (we'll be doing some more work with this later).

Your story for each Asset should be 3 to 6 sentences, 10 sentences at the max. The story should be a real-life situation where your Asset was displayed, utilized, or visible. Or perhaps a story of when you first realized you had this Asset.

For example, if your #1 Asset was *Hard Working,* choose an example of when you displayed that Asset. It is best in a work environment, but that's not a requirement. If you have a good story that is outside of an employee scenario, tell it! The better the story, the more effective you will be.

EXAMPLE OF AN ASSET EXPRESSED AS A NARRATIVE

If one of your Assets was "Easily form deep and meaningful relationships with others," then you might remember *that time*

46

> *at summer camp, when you were 12, and you made friends with everyone in your cabin, and even today stay in touch with 3 of them.*
>
> And that in turn might remind you of *that time, in your first job, when you made friends with your colleagues, and one of them introduced you to espresso, which you initially didn't like, but today love… and another colleague that helped you buy your first car. And you're still in touch with both of them.*
>
> Write that down, in just those kinds of words. You're drafting, not crafting.

Figure 3.2 Example of an Asset expressed as a narrative.

Do you notice how the drily-stated dimension in this example, about forming relationships, came alive when placed in the context of two different stories?

That's your objective. You should end up with a document with each Asset in priority order, and for each Asset at least short story, one snippet that illuminates the Asset (and maybe two very short stories, like the above example).

It is not uncommon for my clients to go back and revise their Asset List, either with new additions or a changed priority, after developing narratives for each Asset. This exercise has a way of unlocking our memories and perhaps loosening our preconceived notions of how we think about our Assets in a genuine way.

Yes, you can write narratives for all of your Assets if you wish, not just the top 10 as specified above.

EXAMPLE OF ASSET LIST WITH A NARRATIVE

1. Asset: Curious about people
I want to know what their story is, figure them out, why are they here right now… why are they in this particular place in time, and why? When I meet someone, I want to know who they are, and how I can best relate to them.

2. Asset: Ambitious
It is important to me to do well. I push pretty hard, and I need external validation. I draw confidence from having won a Fulbright scholarship, or being hired by this prestigious firm, and from attending a well-known grad school. I try hard not to judge this, but I can't deny it.

3. Asset: Can strike up conversation with just about anyone
I like watching people, and wherever I am, if there is an opportunity to connect… I try to do so. I'm not going to randomly talk to you if you're standing in line for a salad, but if we're sitting next to each other on a plane… I really enjoy connecting with people…so I look for opportunities to do so.

Figure 3.3 Example of an Asset List with narratives.

Note that in this example the narrative resembles a stream of consciousness more than a carefully crafted message. Perfect!

There will be an opportunity later for creativity; right now we're intent on not missing any Assets, and understanding better why the Assets matter to you.

And yes, ambition is an Asset, given the right context.

Step 3:
Draft Your Brand Statement

This step should not be rushed. In fact, it is not uncommon for my clients to spend 4 to 6 hours total on this next step, over a period of 2 to 3 weeks. For others, it's easy and flows out of them in 20 minutes. In my own experience, it never seems easy, and it always requires several drafts. Anyone can do it, but it takes some effort.

This is perhaps counter to your intuition, but put away your old paper resume. Do not look at it for this part of the exercise. This process calls for a fresh start, a new way of describing who you really are.

Take the Asset List that you refined, prioritized, and narrated in the previous Step #2 and put it in front of you. If you have it on your computer now, you may want to literally print it out. Then go somewhere quiet where you can reflect—you don't need a computer to write your brand statement.

First write two or three declarative statements that include all of the top 10 Assets you identified. Generally speaking, you'll need two or three paragraphs to do this, with two or three sentences in each paragraph.

Real examples from actual individuals may help illustrate the objective of this exercise:

BRAND STATEMENT EXAMPLE: PASSION

I am a catalyst for change. I create "Ah-ha" experiences in the classroom, uncover gifts not yet recognized, and facilitate guided self-discovery in consultation with social workers in the field, or coaching other facilitators or trainers focused on child welfare and mental health.

What I do best is inspire. Through my stories, you see possibilities emerge and then picture yourself as the hero of that story in which a family comes together, and the village reaches out to help protect a child.

I am drawn like a magnet to difficult conversations in a group, because in transforming the loudest critic, I transform individuals into a committed team working toward a common goal. I am passionate about this work.

Figure 3.4 Passion in a Brand Statement.

Notice that the individual in Figure 3.4 uses declarative statements, highlights her passions, and gives a glimpse of how those passions affect what she loves to do.

Normally I recommend against getting into the *how* and sticking with *what* you do… but by including it, she communicates her passion for her profession.

This is a great personal brand.

BRAND STATEMENT EXAMPLE: BREVITY

I am a product-oriented, execution-focused lateral thinker. Technology and creativity are passions I combine. And early-stage projects are my sweet spot.

Figure 3.5 Brevity in a Brand Statement.

This client (see Figure 3.5) took the assignment literally and pragmatically, and made it very short and direct. Bravo. No attempt to prove or defend: his statements are assertive and declarative.

If you were developing a technology-based product in your startup and you viewed this profile on LinkedIn, I'll bet you would be intrigued by his brand statement. You would want to know more about him.

Perfect.

BRAND STATEMENT EXAMPLE: INCLUDING PERSONAL INTERESTS

My passion is helping companies grow faster by acquiring more customers and developing greater operational expertise.

Technology's potential to reshape use of the world's finite resources drives my fascination with clean tech and sustainability.

A voracious reader, student of great communications, and world traveler, I count Richard Russo, Nancy Duarte, and faraway places like the Galapagos Islands among my favorites.

Figure 3.6 Personal Interests within a Brand Statement.

This example (see Figure 3.6) separates three topics into separate paragraphs, with revealing and candid statements about each topic. Note that unlike the first two brand statement examples, you get a sense of his life beyond his work.

If you're left with questions about that, or his work, then this brand statement is effective. Ideally, you want your viewer to want to more about you; your brand statement should *not* be a comprehensive summary of the whole person.

BRAND STATEMENT EXAMPLE: COMPLEXITY WITH A FOCUS

I work at the intersection of design, technology, and entrepreneurship, building iconic tools for passionate creators to refine and differentiate their craft.

I believe in machines that do real work in the real world. Machines secure intellectual property, manifest their brands physically, create persistent differentiated connections to customers, and improve lives tangibly. Creativity-enabling platforms—for foodies, musicians, builders and artists—inspire customers while accruing profit and loyalty for business.

I enjoy audacious product visions because they are magnets for world-class teams.

Figure 3.7 A Brand Statement with complexity.

The client in Figure 3.7 has a lot to say about his passions, which interact with each other, and as a result his brand statement is complex.

Good—you get a sense for the individual after you read this, and it is clear what he wants to do next, because he tells you directly.

If you are developing products, particularly hardware, you would want to talk to this person to know more.

Mission accomplished.

WHY THESE BRAND STATEMENTS WORK

Each of the clients in these four examples makes a statement about *what they do*—without providing any proof or credibility they can do it, although the implication is that they have done it and are good at it.

Each describes to some degree *why* they do it, or at least asserts that it is their passion. They don't explain how they do it, unless that "how" is not blindingly obvious.

If you're in the same kind of work, you're likely intrigued by what you read. This means you want to know more.

And that means that you are more likely to keep scrolling down the window of your smartphone, or clicking through on your computer, to check out the rest of this individual's LinkedIn Profile.

Bam! That's the objective.

That is why you *don't* attempt to prove your assertions at this point in your LinkedIn Profile. That would take up too much room, and runs the risk (heck, the certainty) that the reader loses interest.

Grab them, be confident and definitive, and they'll keep looking at your profile. Or not.

And this is key: if they're *not* in the same work or *don't* find anything that resonates in your brand statement, then *you haven't lost anything.*

You've made it efficient for them to see that there isn't a fit, and that's not a bad thing. We'll return to this point later.

REFINING YOUR DRAFT

Now you need to refine your brand statement. Attempt to include each of your top 10 Assets identified in Step #2, but don't obsess. If one or two of your Assets just don't fit, leave them out.

Sometimes that's how we refine what is really important to our brand… by drafting it. Don't worry, we have a way to include the Assets not in your brand statement, by placing them in another part of your LinkedIn Profile (more on that in a moment). Not *everything* about you goes in your brand statement!

As you write, your guidelines include:

- Active verbs, not passive. "I lead our chapter of Phi Delta Kappa" rather than "I was inducted into Phi Delta Kappa"
- Show emotion. "I love to…" rather than "Skilled in …"
- Declare, don't prove. "I work at the intersection of…" rather than "With years of experience, I work at the…"
- Minimize adjectives and superlatives. Avoid "As a top-ranked and deeply experienced…"

The key to drafting your brand statement is to confidentially declare what you love to do. *Own it.*

Set your draft aside. We'll be returning to it later.

Step 4:
Build Credibility With Your Life Experience

Print out your current paper resume or C.V. You probably thought it was complete, but it likely isn't.

Now start marking it up with a pen or pencil to *add* experience that you have gained that wasn't necessarily part of a job. A traditional resume documents job experience, and relegates non-job experience to a different part of the resume… or omits it completely, left to the persistence of the interviewer to tease it out of the candidate. The **Experience** section of your LinkedIn Profile is going to be different.

Include businesses you've helped, volunteer positions, and classes you've taken—seminars, workshops, anything that helps illuminate you and your Assets. You are transforming your job history into your life history. You'll see why in a moment.

THE FACTS
For each life experience, you need to write down
- The name of the organization or employer
- A one or two sentence description of what the organization does.
- Your title (or *role* if titles were not applicable)
- Month/Year start
- Month/Year end

You can skip the exercise of describing what the organization does, if it is obvious to everyone. For example, United Airlines, Apple Computer, et al. But if in doubt, explain it. For instance, if you built military airplanes at Boeing, explain that. Most readers would assume that Boeing only makes civilian airliners. *Just keep it short.*

NARRATIVE

And then for each experience, write 1 or 2 sentences about what you did, in the context of what the organization *needed from you.*

This is hard because it's hard to be brief. The old paper resume format encouraged details in each job title, with laundry lists of accomplishments. That's not the objective. Tell the *bare minimum* of what you did… because you're saving room to tell us *why it mattered.*

After you tell us (briefly) what you did, then tell us a story about using one of your Assets in this job or role.

Or tell us a story about how you first realized how important your Asset was to you in this role. *Tell us about the use of your Asset in this role.*

Do *not* list everything you did in that role. Do *not* list all of your accomplishments and achievements in that role. This is not a resume. Instead, give us a story.

Resist the temptation to provide a laundry list of accomplishments—or worse, official "responsibilities" pulled from the bureaucratic job description of the position. Don't do it. It is boring. Nobody cares.

You're looking for a short, terse "story" that *proves your Asset.*

You're attempting to follow the writer's maxim: *show, don't tell* (see Figure 3.8 below and on the next page for a specific example).

EXPERIENCE EXAMPLE

If one of your Assets was *"I love helping people learn, to see the light in something they didn't understand before."*

Then you might change the experience from your paper resume from this:

"Marketing Director: supervised 3 staff with an annual budget of $1.3 million, exceeding goals set for the business unit by 133%"

to something like this:

"Marketing Director: exceeded goals, largely by helping team members realize their potential, which helped me realize that I love to help people learn and improve."

Figure 3.8 Proof of your Asset.

Don't get me wrong. If the person in Figure 3.8 is applying for a job in marketing, she may well need to explain in an interview about her experience with a small staff and a $1.3 million budget.

But the details of that experience are *not* part of her brand and don't belong in her LinkedIn Profile.

But her Asset of "helping people learn" absolutely is a key part of your brand, and *she should definitely* tell that story.

For your personal brand, you want to provide "proof" for your Asset, in the form of a story. In the context of your brand, the reader doesn't really care about your budget, the number of your reports, or the metric of 133%... and even if they did, the space available in LinkedIn (or a traditional paper resume) prohibits you from providing enough context for the reader to understand the significance of this.

This is one of the reasons why a good interviewer might spot that snippet in your paper resume, and ask about it: "So what did you learn when you were marketing director?" or "What did you like best about being a marketing director?" because *they're trying to understand you, not your accomplishments.*

You wouldn't want to make them work for it in an interview, so don't do that in your LinkedIn Profile.

Connect the dots of your experience together for the viewer, so they don't have to interview you to learn this about you.

You may have realized by now that this exercise is quite similar to Step #2, when you wrote narratives for each of your Assets.

That was the warm up, this is the real thing.

Make each life experience really count—what did you learn, what did you discover, what did you tap… that made the experience worth-while?

And this is a good place to illuminate an Asset that didn't fit into your Brand Statement draft; put it in the context of your life experience.

It is often helpful to work this process in the order your life has unfolded. In other words, start with your first position long ago and tell that story. Then tell the next one, moving along the path of your life.

Do this for each role you have listed in your life experience. Perhaps an example will help (see Figure 3.9):

PAPER RESUME EXAMPLE

Training and Instructional Design—State University (2012–2015)
Developed computer-based training for social workers to support their work with LGBTQ youth.

Training—Home for Children (2007–2012)
Developed curriculum and worked with other team members to deliver to various agencies.

President—TWO Learning Connection (2005–2007)
Founded consulting company and provided e-learning and classroom instruction to 5 different agencies over 20-months.

Training and Curriculum Coordinator—System of Care (2002–2005)
Helped develop a computer-based training program as well as delivering curriculum to instructors across seven counties, eventually serving 500 individuals.

Community Outreach—Family Resource Center (2000– 2002)
Worked directly with clients and managed a challenging caseload.

Supervisor Intensive Case Management—Rocky Mountain
Center (1994–2000)
Supervised team and designed programs, as well as working
directly with clients.

Figure 3.9 Example of an old-school Resume.

While the version in Figure 3.9 lacks detail for each role, this is
highly typical of what is seen in most LinkedIn Profiles. In fact, I usually see even less information—just the organization's name, and the title
of the job.

Now let's see this old-school resume transformed into life experience draft, highlighting Assets and providing credibility for the assertions made in the brand statement (see Figure 3.10).

LIFE EXPERIENCE
IN SUPPORT OF A BRAND STATEMENT

Training and Instructional Design
State University
2012 – 2015
The Center for Family and Community Engagement has a clear
focus on bringing the best research together with the experiences of family and youth to the forefront of every project. Projects
with this team allowed me to deepen my engagement skills and
build my capacity for excellent scholarship. My favorite product
was the development of an asynchronous computer-based training—Learning to Support, Empower and Include LGBTQ
Youth in Substitute Care. This curriculum is unique
in its scope and format. The design and development process
stretched my existing skills to build the learning scaffolding
needed to approach and under- stand a complex and often

contentious topic. I also had the distinct pleasure of acting as a mentor to professional colleagues.

Training, Consultant, Instructional Design
Home for Children
2007 – 2012
This team took partnership, excellent customer service, and performance improvement to a whole new level. We were committed to bringing our best in support of state and local child protection teams through the work of implementing Differential Response and improving family engagement. Through collaboration across different state cultures I learned that there are many right ways to accomplish the goal. I also worked on the development and delivery of a curriculum called Building Awareness and Cultural Competency. Navigating difficult conversations about stereotypes, biases, and prejudice allowed me to hone my skills in appreciative inquiry and guided self-discovery.

President and Founder
TWO Learning Connection, Inc
2005 – 2007
My first foray as an entrepreneur. This was an incredible opportunity to learn flexibility and accountability and to grow my instructional design and facilitation skills. Customer service was key to survival. I was an independent provider of e-learning, class- room facilitation, and consulting services to private and public entities.

Training and Curriculum Coordinator
System of Care
2002 – 2005
This group did a ground-breaking thing by developing a computer-based training that would outlive the grant. This was still a pretty new idea in the early 2000s. I led the process from

beginning to end, and the result supported continued learning for years past the life of the grant.

I took on a new role as the Training and Curriculum Coordinator for a seven-county demonstration site. We were charged with streamlining services, improving collaboration and functionality across all child and family service delivery areas. This project is where I found a new passion—facilitation and curriculum design. I learned a lot about designing and delivering instructor-led curricula by providing training to over 500 people from diverse organizations. I worked closely with family advocates as well as service providers at all phases of the project.

Community Outreach and Family Education
Family Resource Center
2000 – 2002
When my youngest son was born, I took a position with a local family resource center so I would have more access to him. It turned out to be a cornerstone career move. Working in a voluntary, community-based, grant-funded environment with some of the same families I had previously served in a mandated, agency-led system had a profound impact on my thinking about what it means to be in service. It also marks a shift to focusing on the wisdom of families and a close connection with family advocacy and peer mentorship.

Supervisor Intensive Case Management
Rocky Mountain Center
1994 – 2000
My work in the arena of children's mental health began in a group home in Georgia where I quickly unlearned most of what I thought I knew about youth and mental illness. I found out I like teenagers quite a bit. When I moved to the mountains of North Carolina to start my own family, I went to work at a local

mental health center doing one-on-one work focused on keeping kids in the least restrictive environment possible. In a short span of time I was supervising a team and redesigning the program. I was then recruited to lead an intensive case management team in the same organization.

Work with Young and School Age Children
Early Career
1988 – 1994
Early in my career I worked with young children. As the lead teacher of a 3-year-old classroom, I went through a rigorous accreditation process with an Atlanta day care center. I loved this job! I still remember many of their faces. It took me years to let go of the puppets I made for singalong and nap-time. Later I worked as a teacher's assistant at a Montessori school where I fell in love with the transformational power of learning. I ran their after-school program and designed the first summer camp the school ever offered so I got to start from scratch. The summer camp was my first design work as well as my first experience with supervision.

Figure 3.10 Rewrite of an old-school resume into a Life Experience to support a Brand Statement

Obviously, in the second version of the life experience, the narrative of each position is longer and more descriptive. But note that the description is almost always written in the style of a story, as if the writer is talking directly to you.

She "connects the dots" of her work in each job together, and bridges one work experience to another. For example, at the Rocky Mountain Center *(the names of the organizations have been changed for privacy)* she notes "where I quickly unlearned most of what I thought I knew about youth and mental illness."

She even adds an additional "experience" entry that wasn't even in her old-school resume, illuminating how she fell in love with learning.

This is not what you would put in a traditional resume, but placed here, it draws the reader in and the admission strongly reinforces that our writer is dedicated to learning. One of her Assets.

Note that at one position, she "found a new passion—facilitation and curriculum design." This is the kind of color you would generally only uncover in an interview, but in your first view of this profile, you're getting a sense of what is important to her.

This is key, if you are considering this person for a facilitation responsibility. She's been loving it for at least 10 years already!

Also note that her first "job" is a collection of jobs, with the detail of title, organization, exact dates and so forth omitted. Nobody cares about those details. By omitting these, she has instead summarized for us *what was relevant* about those early years, and it provides a sense of how she developed her Assets in designing curriculum, supervising, and loving the power of learning.

So many of us have had similar transformational moments in our budding careers, usually kept hidden, even during the interview process.

Consider for a moment how significant it is—that you can get a well-rounded sense of this individual, a glimpse into her personal life (she has a family, she loves being in service) and "proof" of how she has been able to accomplish what she has done in her professional life.

All without knowing exactly where she worked, since I've obscured the actual identity of the organizations! Almost an anti-resume, but far more effective in quickly understanding who she is, what she can do, and what she loves doing.

Finally, it is important to see that the Life Experience goes hand-in-hand with the Brand Statement, so let's take a look at her brand statement (see Figure 3.11 on the next page).

BRAND STATEMENT EXAMPLE:
ALIGNED WITH LIFE EXPERIENCE NARRATIVE

I am an architect of learning. As a facilitator and instructional designer, I think creatively. I provide the instructional scaffolding needed to support a thorough and engaging learning environment.

I can support a group through difficult conversations, managing the tension when a topic is charged. I bring compassion, wit, and experience to the learning process.

I have a passion for people and the 'Aha' experience. I believe the collective wisdom is greater than what individuals bring. I love uncovering and sharing that wisdom in a group.

Figure 3.11 The brand statement that is supported by the rewritten Life Experience history.

Now go back and read through her experience. See that she has made assertions about what she can do and what she loves to do in her brand statement, and backed that up with a narrative in her life experience that provides the credibility, and many more details.

This is an excellent personal brand.

Step 5:
Refine Your Brand Statement

Now go back to your brand statement drafted in Step #3. I don't want to beat a dead horse, but I've seen over and over again in my clients' efforts on their brand statements—that your work on the Life Experience section will change your expectations for your brand statement.

So let's go back now and review it, in the light of your Life Experience. Remember that you want to draft an easy-to-read, declarative statement of who you are. This should be done with a focus on your professional life, but not necessarily exclusively.

In other words, you can include your personal life, your family life, your charitable work…whatever helps to *define you* to a stranger.

Do not leave out Assets that help illuminate who you are and what you love to do.

What does the Brand Statement include?

The answer is different for each person, because we are all so different, but also so that you are differentiated.

Our guiding principle is authenticity. Describe the authentic you, because frankly that is not only the natural, but also most likely to be unique.

- Describe the work you love.
- Summarize what you offer to the world.
- Name your Assets (but no more than 10).

What does the Brand Statement *not* include?

- *Don't* describe the job you want.
- *Don't* summarize your work history.

Tell the reader what you do, not what you've done (the **Experience** section you just created in Step #4 will tell them what you've done).

BREVITY IN THE BRAND STATEMENT

After following the first four steps of The Method, you may have written a lengthy brand statement, attempting to capture everything that is important to you. That's good, but that's why we called it a draft. You will almost surely need to edit for brevity.

Why keep it short?

The reality is that most people will read your brand statement while holding their smartphone, waiting for their latte at a coffee shop. Or while listening to you talk in a meeting. It needs to be punchy, short, and readable.

How short? If you read it aloud, in a normal tone of voice and a relaxed cadence, it should be *less than 15 seconds*. That's usually 5 to 7 sentences of normal length, at most.

Reading it aloud is a great test.

It should sound natural and use words and terms that you would actually use in a conversation, say at a cocktail party. Forget the business correspondence style of writing, and write like you really talk.

When someone reads it on their phone, it will play in their head, and it needs to be that easy and natural to "read." It should "sound" like you. So test it with your own natural voice.

YOU DON'T HAVE MUCH ROOM

Since *more than half* of the people who view your profile will do so *on a smartphone*, you should check your profile on an actual smartphone even as you compose your profile on a desktop or laptop computer. This will help you adjust your expectations.

In the example in Figure 3.12 on the next page, I've taken an image of my smartphone screen, using the LinkedIn mobile app to display one of my LinkedIn connections (one of my clients).

As you can see, my client got just three and a half sentences of his brand statement visible in the LinkedIn Summary.

Of course, smartphones are getting larger (this image is of an ancient iPhone 5) so this is a bit of a worst-case scenario, but you really shouldn't count on more real estate than this.

You don't have much room to grab your viewer, so keep it short.

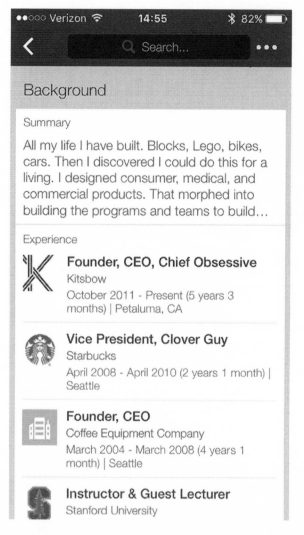

Figure 3.12 Example of a typical LinkedIn Profile on a smartphone. Not much room!

GOLD STANDARD

And there's another reason to keep it short: One of the most useful purposes for the brand statement is so that it can be *repeated*. As in, repeated by others.

If you keep it short enough, memorable enough, and direct enough… any reader of your brand statement could potentially tell others about you.

Because you didn't ask them to remember too much.

This is a key indicator of the perfect pitch, which I've written about elsewhere. Great brands are talked about, and passed on to others, constantly.

Make it easy for your reader to pass your brand statement along. When you *overhear someone else* accurately and completely repeating your brand statement, then you will have met the gold standard.

TAKE THE TIME TO MAKE IT BRIEF

I will caution you that as hard as the previous exercise of rewriting your work history was, this exercise of editing for brevity may be even more difficult.

As Blaise Pascal, the French mathematician and philosopher said, *"I would have written you a shorter letter, but I didn't have the time."*

Assume you will need to revise your brand statement with several drafts. Perhaps this challenge will be better understood with a few examples.

In the next example (see Figure 3.13), the individual has a formal design background and relevant credentials, and is currently an entrepreneur *(this is the client illuminated in the iPhone example above).*

BRAND STATEMENT EXAMPLE: LEAVES YOU WANTING TO KNOW MORE

All my life I have built. Blocks, Lego, bikes, cars. Then I discovered I could do this for a living. I designed consumer, medical, and commercial products.

That morphed into building the programs and teams to build products, and then, I built a company. It was the hardest thing I'd ever done, but it was been the most rewarding, fun, and downright amazing experience.

I worked with our acquirer, a large public company, for about two years and then took time off to enjoy family and work on "what's next." Now, what's next is here: my new company!

Figure 3.13 A Brand Statement that makes you want to know more -- a motive for keeping it brief.

In this example, we're reading a narrative, a snippet of what is surely a rich and detailed story. No titles, no technical accomplishments, not a laundry list of job roles.

The result? You have a sense of the guy, and you want to know more. Perfect, just what he needs for his new venture.

The next example is more challenging, with a more complicated story with the added challenge of combining years of volunteer work with a previous career, and providing emphasis for a new career (see Figure 3.14).

BRAND STATEMENT EXAMPLE:
THE RELEVANCE OF NON-PROFIT WORK

For many years, I researched how a virus infects a cell by specific proteins and how this interaction regulates the cell and the immune response to the infection. I divided my time between bench work (experiments!), drafting peer-review papers, and securing 100% of the funding for my lab through grant awards.

Later, I applied my proven grant writing skills to establish and expand art and science programs for several nonprofit organizations. I built an elementary school science education portfolio starting with a Science Fair (which had 100-fold increase in participation in 2 years) that grew to a Day of Science with all 650+ students participating in hands on science supported by my collaborations with University, Science Museum, and Community Organizations.

My passion for understanding processes and translating these ideas into successful projects either on the cellular, technical, or interpersonal level has led me to a broader desire to protect inventions through patent prosecution.

Figure 3.14 Placing volunteer work in the context of a previous career, and in support of a new career.

While this brand statement can't be short, and also uses scientific jargon (such as "peer-review" and "protect inventions") it is an authentic statement of what she can do, why she did it, and what she is doing now.

By the way, she also has a long list of publications, patents, and other credentials in her C.V. typical of an academic researcher—none of which are referenced in this brand statement. Good. The rest of her LinkedIn Profile will do that job for her.

A third example (Figure 3.15) is a consultant who works with both small and large organizations, but knows that he performs best when it is early stage.

BRAND STATEMENT EXAMPLE: BRIEF AND EFFICIENT

For 15+ years I've built impetus for early-stage companies and programs. I thrive on diving into projects that involve a high degree of ambiguity.

I apply well-tested pattern-matching abilities to forge partnerships, establish supportive ecosystems, gain early customer sales, and help focus business model/product definition—typically with a minimum of marketing support and often with only demos/prototypes.

I've done this successfully with big ideas hatched by others as well as with my own initiatives. And I'm as comfortable launching funded startups as I am driving new programs within established organizations.

Figure 3.15 Brief but also efficient.

This is one of the most efficient brand statements I've yet encountered—he's told you exactly what he *does well* and what he *loves to do.*

Many readers don't need his Assets, but because he's so crisp, the ones that do will recognize their future team member right away.

And even the viewers that don't need him for their organization are more likely to remember this short, brief statement… and as a result, are more likely to refer him to people who do need him.

Everybody wins.

TOTAL FAIL

For a final example of brand statements, I've chosen an individual who is accomplished, connected, and has great credentials, including graduate degrees from the best schools.

He is an impressive Silicon Valley industry executive; we'll call him Mr. CEO/CTO to protect his identity.

I don't know Mr. CEO/CTO and he hasn't been through my method to craft a brand statement. So we're going to pick on him a bit as an example of *how not to do it.*

His profile on LinkedIn has one of the longest **Summary** sections I've ever found, demonstrating the opposite of the brevity I urge you to use.

He has literally listed his career in his summary, rather than authoring an authentic brand statement (see Figure 3.16).

SUMMARY
Technology leader with 20 years experience in startups, entrepreneurship, venture capital, product management, and
engineering.
Past roles as CEO, CTO, product management executive, and
venture capitalist.

EXPERIENCE
VP Product at XYZ - the original fin-tech company. We help
over 800,000 employees manage their $100 billion in retirement
assets.
CTO at ABC - Ad-tech company serving publishers
EIR at VENTUREA - Creating new entrepreneurial ventures
with VENTUREA founder in online advertising, mobile applications and consumer internet
CEO of ACME - Ad-tech company selling ad targeting technology to DSPs, ad exchanges and networks and other participants in the ad ecosystem.
CTO of AWESOME Inc. - One of the largest distributed
media networks on the Internet, reaching nearly 20% of the US
audience.

Passion for:
• Commercializing and launching innovative technology in
  operationally sound and scalable fashion leveraging agile and
  lean best practices
• Building hyper growth organizations and navigating market
  shifts
Notables experiences: Venture Capital - Five years as venture
capitalist investing in technology. Technology Startups - Entrepreneur, manager, and individual contributor within early-
stage technology companies.

*Figure 3.16 Total Fail of a LinkedIn **Summary** Section.*

I could hardly make myself read it all the way through the first time —and I *was motivated* to read it so that I could include it in this book.

His profile is a list of titles and company names, along with accomplishments that are not placed in context. It doesn't help that he uses industry buzzwords to describe his "passion", which makes the shallow narrative even less interesting and distinct.

And all of this text is in his **Summary** section of his LinkedIn Profile—this isn't even the **Experience** section. There's even more mind-numbing detail there. Sigh.

If you made it all the way through, all you are likely to retain is that he's worked in a lot of jobs and has accomplished a great deal, according to him. That is a brand statement of a sort, but it's not an effective one. It is not unique. It is not credible.

To be fair, if I hadn't changed the names of the companies to protect his identity, you *might* be impressed. But imagine the possibilities if he had truly revealed who he is through a true brand statement, rather than relying on us to be impressed by a laundry list of his employers.

And as we consider whether to include him in a business relationship in the future, to make future plans… not only do we not know who he is, we don't even know what he loves to do, or what specific Assets he uses to win and offers to others.

Even if we're impressed by his laundry list, we're left a bit empty. He's missed the opportunity to grab us, to tell us a story that motivates us to keep scrolling down through the experience… and leaving us with the desire to get in touch with him to hear the rest of the story.

And this failure illustrates a key point: your brand should inspire the reader to make a human connection. It is an age-old adage that *no resume ever got a job* (only an interview).

Don't make the same mistake when defining *your* brand—offer intrigue and interest, show a glimpse of the authentic you, but don't lay everything out on the table. This is another reason for brevity.

Step 6:
Create An Awesome Headline
For Your Brand

Now we're going to bite off one of the hardest parts of the six-step method: sum it all up in one or two words, perhaps three at the most.

What word or phrase best captures *you?* What is the core of your brand? Peeking ahead to **Part 4** of this book, you will be using this in your profile. In fact, your headline will introduce you to the world!

This is one of the best features of LinkedIn: a single word or short phrase that summarizes the authentic you—called your **Professional Headline**.

As you look around LinkedIn, you'll see the **Professional Headline** used very effectively by savvy LinkedIn users.

And best of all, you choose it. No one has to approve it. If you have a job, your current employer has no say. It is not your current title. It is not what you thought you went to school to learn. It's what you are now, in this moment.

Brevity is best: one word, two words, maybe three words.

Make it count, make it memorable like these examples (see Figure 3.17).

GOOD EXAMPLES

- Startup Guy, Product Guy
- Writer
- Momentum-builder for early initiatives
- Sharing Economy & Marketplace Consultant
- Serial Entrepreneur
- Grand Poohbah
- Venture Capitalist, Technology Entrepreneur

- Author, Teacher, Explainer
- Chief Obsessive
- Entrepreneur, Instigator, Author, Founder

Figure 3.17 Great examples of Professional Headlines.

Brainstorm on this, and try to choose something that says clearly and effectively what you are… and if possible, make it memorable.

Do not use your current job title. Not only is it boring, but it misses the opportunity to communicate precisely who you are (see Figure 3.18). *Be authentic.*

MISSED OPPORTUNITIES

- CMO
- Software Architect
- General Manager
- CEO
- Marketing Team Leader
- Public Sector Account Manager

Figure 3.18 Missed opportunities for Professional Headlines.

You may find it interesting that all of the "good" examples I provide here are plucked from my network, and nearly are all successful marketers who have succeeded in their work many times. That's not a coincidence.

Wrapping It Up

At this point you have three working documents: a great **Professional Headline** with a succinct **Brand Statement;** an **Asset List;** and your **Life Experience.**

Like my client the architect who loves aviation but didn't think of it as an Asset, check one more time for hidden Assets that aren't yet reflected in your Life Experience.

Look through your list of awards and recognition, and see if any of these demonstrate or prove an Asset you've identified. Perhaps you've missed one that you want to illuminate?

Remember that the underlying philosophy of this entire exercise is authenticity. Are you being authentic?

If you've done the Brand Statement and Life Experience documents in **Word** (or **Google Docs**), this is a good time to carefully examine both documents for typos and misspellings. Did you say "to" when you meant to type "too"? "There" instead of "Their"? Fire House instead of Fire Hose? Remember that spell-checkers have limitations, and consider asking someone else to proofread your drafts looking for mispellings. Make one last check, as it is easier to do it here than later.

This is the heft of your personal brand, and although we're definitely not finished yet, this is the lion's share of the work, the hardest part is over.

I often encourage clients to share these documents with someone else they trust to be direct and helpful, and get their feedback.

And then it's back to work, as we push through the rest of the process of creating a profile on the LinkedIn service.

PART 4:
Loading LinkedIn

Art is about building a new foundation, not just laying something on top of what's already there.

~Prince

AT THIS POINT YOU HAVE a distinctive professional headline, a brand statement with punch, along with a chronologically-ordered life experience, narrated to reveal your Assets.

The hard work of drawing out what you really want, describing what you've done that matters, and documenting it in a text document is not only complete, but carefully spell-checked and reviewed for accuracy.

The next step is to load this text, and other information, into the LinkedIn system to create your brand presence.

And we will take careful steps to ensure your brand is presented in a way that you intend. It is time to take a look at the big picture of your brand presence.

The Framework of an Effective Profile

The well-used metaphor of peeling off the layers of an onion comes to mind, as we consider your headline (1 to 3 words), your brand statement (15 or so seconds when read aloud) and your life experience documenting your Assets in use over the years (and decades). While the tradition-al resume certainly uses that "onion" structure, your LinkedIn presence is more complex than the onion metaphor can support.

Your brand is both broad and deep, with several dimensions. This is a good problem to have, because each person reading this book and using this method will have different Assets and varied experience. The LinkedIn service provides a structure that accommodates those differences.

I recommend you view the "big picture" of the LinkedIn framework this way:

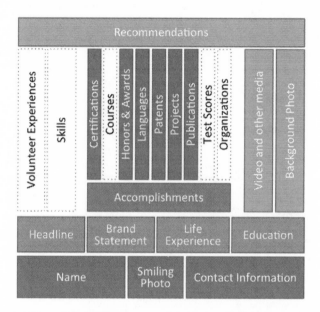

*Figure 4.1 Your LinkedIn presence consists of a variety of Sections, each requiring thoughful choice for inclusion. Each profile will vary, given each person's Assets and experience. (**The blocks with dotted outlines indicate Sections that should be avoided by all users**).*

Your LinkedIn Profile *isn't* your full presence on LinkedIn. In **Part 6**, we'll address the other important aspects of your presence: the number of connections, your status posts, following high-profile individuals, and the conduct of inviting others to connect (and accepting invitations). Our focus in this **Part 4** is on *your profile.*

We will examine each of the sections and blocks in the framework, and guide you in utilizing each of those sections and blocks.

It cannot be overemphasized that the inclusion of a section or block must be guided *by the value* of the inclusion, versus the cost of creating an ever-larger and ever-fatter LinkedIn Profile.

Large profiles will not be effective. As we've discussed previously, more than half of all interested parties will use a smartphone or be pressed for time, or multitasking (or all three) while skimming your information. By necessity, the overarching consideration is that the overall profile be as short as possible.

A good guideline: if you are tempted to load something into your LinkedIn Profile that is not consistent with this framework, don't do it.

Unlike your traditional old school resume, *do not* list every single possible thing, in hopes of triggering interest or connection. If your profile is too long, the reader will never actually see it, so including anything "extra" is irrelevant.

If the reader can't easily skim your LinkedIn presence and come away with a sense of the authentic you, specifically of your brand statement... then we've failed.

Keep your top-level goals clear, and work within this framework. Rules of thumb to apply:

- Avoid laundry lists (although a punchy bullet list can be OK)
- Go deep on Assets, particularly passions
- Avoid going long on accomplishments
- Superlatives and adjectives should be used sparingly, if at all
- Breadth is truly great (we're all complicated) but don't confuse it for comprehensive list-making

To help you with this, I've already outlined some of the sections and blocks in the overall framework *with dotted lines*. With rare exception, *I do not recommend any reader of this book to utilize these sections or blocks.* Either you won't need them, or there is a better way to provide that content.

We'll go through each section and block, and explain why and when you might use it for your LinkedIn presence.

By the way, you can't really do this on a phone, and it is challenging on a tablet. I recommend a laptop or desktop computer, preferably with two displays. Put your open documents from **Part 3** on one of the dislays, and open the LinkedIn service on the other display.

Be sure **Notify My Network** is off *(you should have turned it off during Action #1 in Part 2 of this book)* and if you are unsure, revisit that section to be sure you've done this correctly.

The Foundation

The foundation of the framework is **your name,** the right **photo of you** and your **contact information.**

This is how interested parties will find you, recognize you, and contact you. Search engines will present your name from LinkedIn in their results.

See Figure 4.2 for a conceptual view of this foundation, below.

Figure 4.2 Your name, photo and contact info is the most basic level of your foundation of your LinkedIn Profile.

If you haven't already done so, let's start editing these three blocks. First, open your profile for editing. You can do this by clicking on "me" on the top ribbon, and then click on "view profile" (which is highlighted in blue).

Now click on the "pen" icon on the right side of the top of your profile.

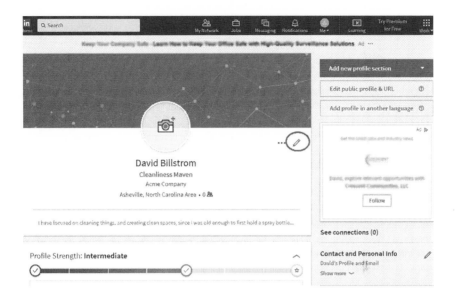

Figure 4.3 Start editing your profile.

You should see a form with various fields, some blank and some with information you've already provided, such as your name. The form should look like Figure 4.4 on the next page.

YOUR NAME

The first item that you may need to edit is your name, even though you already specified your name when you opened your LinkedIn account.

Use your "real" name. You might assume that this is obvious, but I've learned that it isn't. Use the name you use in your profession.

Don't use your legal name, if it differs from the name your colleagues know. When they search for you, which name will they use? If you're Jerry, use Jerry, not your legal name Jerald.

Don't use a family name that is rarely used in practice. If your mom is the only one who calls you Robert, and all of your colleagues know you as Bob, go with Bob.

Figure 4.4 The form for your profile.

You are not filling out a job application for a government agency, with the requirement that you certify your legal name. You're not applying for a job, where they need to check your background or financial credit status. You are creating your personal brand. If your colleagues know you as Dave not David, then use Dave. Use your real name.

NAMES CHANGES AND MAIDEN NAME

Many people have had at least one name change in their life, for a variety of reasons. I recommend that you simply use your current name, but add your previous name in parenthesis—for example, "Sharon (Jehlen) Purvis." This allows those looking for you to find your profile with either your current name, Sharon Purvis, or your prior name, Sharon Jehlen. If you do this, be sure to test it by searching for yourself using both names.

You can Save this form now *(we'll come back to it again soon to finish with the other fields, but first we need to finish the foundation for your frame-work).*

With your profile visible again in front of you, let's move to the next block in your foundation: your photo.

YOUR PHOTO

If you haven't already chosen a great photo and loaded it in, now is the time to do this as well *(see Action #5 in Part 2 of this book for specific advice for a good photo of you).*

Save your change to your photo, and find the section on the screen "Contact and Personal Info" -- it should look like Fig. 4.5 below.

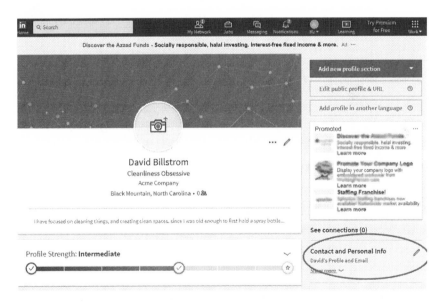

Figure 4.5 Find the "pen" icon for editing the Contact and Personal Info on the far right of your screen.

CONTACT INFORMATION

Some readers may cringe, but I strongly suggest that you provide your direct phone number and your work and/or personal email address. The whole point of your brand is to be known, and to be contacted by your colleagues. Why create a great brand, and then make it hard to reach you for a direct conversation?

This may generate more email spam or marketing phone calls, but in my experience the avenues for that kind of abuse are more numerous elsewhere than LinkedIn (in other words, I'm going to get that anyway). I'd rather that I can be contacted by my connections, than reduce the abuse by a small percentage.

Obviously this advice is context dependent; if you are concerned about specific individuals or a class of individuals, then you may want to remain difficult to contact—which by default will force would-be contacts to use the LinkedIn email system (called **InMail**).

For your connections on LinkedIn, I strongly recommend you provide a suitable email address and phone number (office phone number at a minimum, but consider your mobile number too) and a messenger handle (many are supported, so choose the ones that you will actually use).

I would leave off the physical address unless you have a retail business.

If you don't offer these contact fields in your profile, you're not realizing one of the substantial advantages of LinkedIn: keeping all of your professional contacts up to date on how to reach you.

And by all means provide your website. If you have more than one, knock yourself out and list them all... this may help with SEO (search engine optimization) at your website. No downside to more visitors on your website, especially for free!

Save your work, and you've laid the foundation for your framework. The next layer for your foundation is your **Headline, Brand Statement, Life Experience,** and **Education** (see Figure 4.6 on the next page).

Figure 4.6 The next layer of your foundation is your Headline, Brand
Statement, Life Experience, and Education.

To start on this next layer, open your profile for editing again, clicking on the "pen" icon to the right of your name. You should see the form
again, as in Figure 4.7 below.

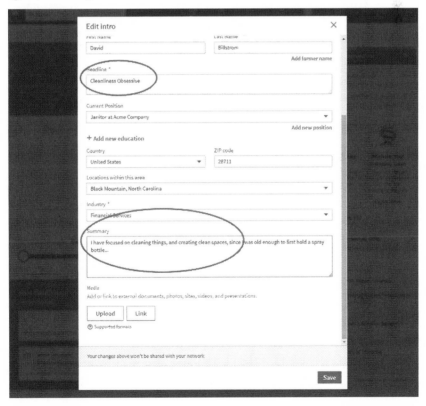

Figure 4.7 Enter your Headline and Brand Statement (in Summary)

HEADLINE

Take the headline you worked so hard to refine, and enter it in the appropriate field of the form (just below your name). You should be able to simply type this in, since it is only a short phrase, right?

BRAND STATEMENT

From your working document, copy your Brand Statement and then paste it into the LinkedIn field labeled **Summary** (towards the bottom of the form) in Figure 4.7.

Feel free to fine-tune the text in your Brand Statement, and in particular experiment with how your use of veritcal "white space" makes the copy easier to read.

LinkedIn doesn't give us any formatting ability such as underline, bold or italic, so you are limited in what you can do to make the text easy to read. This is another reason for keeping your brand statement brief and effective—not a wall of undifferentiated text that the viewer is forced to plow through without the benefit of formatting.

EDUCATION

Click on "Add new education" and you will get a form (see Figure 4.8). Fill in the field for your degree and institution. You will notice that the form attempts to "help" by offering institutions based on the name you enter—take advantage of this, because it provides a link to a reader to the institution, as well as a color logo.

Also consider whether you want to enter the dates of attendance. You do not need to do this, but if you do, understand that almost every business person will attempt to estimate your age based on the date of your undergraduate degree. Ageism is a problem, from both the perspective of being "too young" and sometimes "too old."

I realize that this advice is counter to the philosophy of this book: authenticity. But depending upon your industry, it may be a real factor to consider.

I recommend *skipping* **Field of Study, Grade,** and **Activities and Societies**—unless your activities and societies could illuminate a

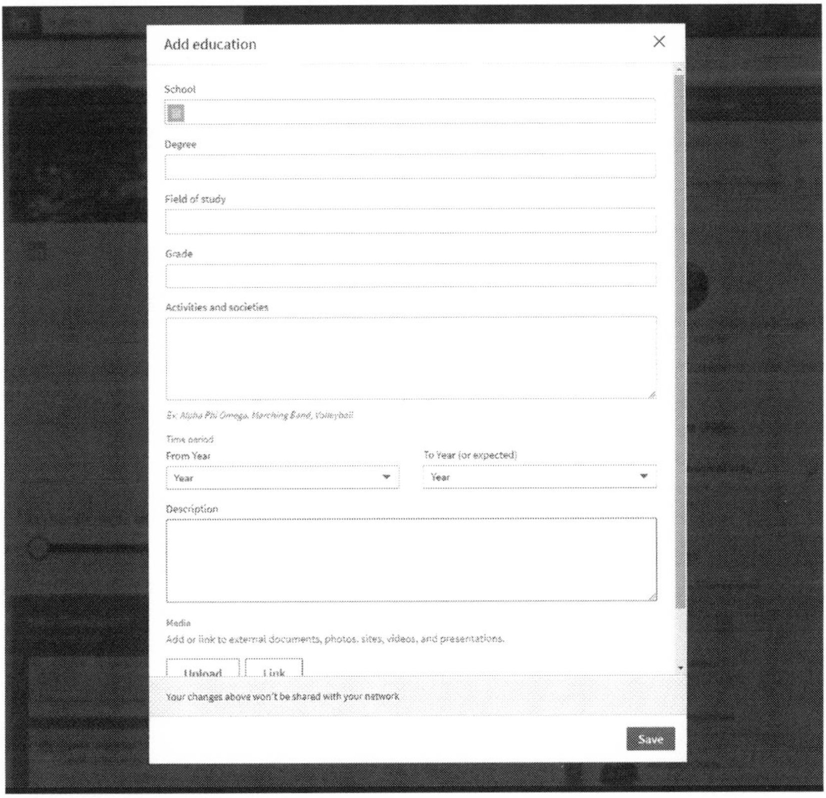

*Figure 4.8 Clicking on **Add Education** should present this form. Be thoughtful about filling in these fields, similar to the entries in the **Experience** Section.*

key Asset of your brand. Otherwise, leave them blank; they're not required. They don't illuminate your Assets. Less is more.

Consider including your high school in your **Education** section if the experience (such as swim team or track), education achievements, or the institution itself played a key role in one or more of the Assets you identified in **Part 3** of this book.

In my case, I include my high school because the Jesuit instructors there are part of a global presence of universities and secondary schools that combine classical studies with religious theology, focusing on academic excellence (since the 16th Century). Because more than one of my own Assets are a direct result of my time with the Jesuits, I include this prep school in my own **Education** section.

You may also want to consider certain workshops and clinics for inclusion in the **Education** section, not only your college and graduate school. These should be given the same test for relevance to your identified Assets.

Most importantly, for each entry in the **Education** section do *not list what you did* or your GPA.

Instead, provide a 1- or 2-sentence narrative of how the experience illuminated one of your Assets, *just as you did for employment positions* when drafting your Life Experience. Put this narrative in the description field for each **Education** entry.

LIFE EXPERIENCE

For this portion of the work, it is very helpful to use two computer displays—one display open with your working documents, and the other display open on the LinkedIn service. You have a lot of copy/paste work to do.

To get started, move your cursor to the **Experience** area of your LinkedIn Profile. You should see a "+" symbol in the upper-right corner. Click on this to get the form similar to the one in Figure 4.9 *(note that the icons may vary in different browsers on different computers)*.

For each "position" in your life experience document, enter the *role* you have previously determined into the "Title" field. Remember that in many situations it is more helpful if you use a descriptive word or phrase for your role… *instead* of a precisely-worded formal title.

For instance, at Intel Corporation I held at least 10 different job titles over 7 years: *Technical Marketing Engineer* (my original job offer letter), *Marketing Engineer, Project Manager, Marketing Manager, International Product Manager, International Marketing Manager, Program Manager, Artificial Intelligence Program Manager, Partner Manager, Product Marketing Engineer, Senior Product Marketing Engineer,* and so on.

You already know what I'm going to tell you: nobody cares.

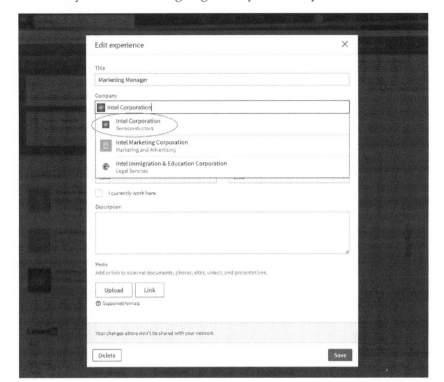

*Figure 4.9 The form for your experience, with a field for "Company"
pre-populated with company names. See if yours is already here.*

There is small chance that Intel even has that original offer letter
in their files, 30 years later. So my formal title is not only irrelevant, but
difficult to verify. It does not help my brand to give an excruciating tour
through my time at Intel, with every reorganization and tour of duty.

So I chose two titles that were descriptive of my roles at Intel, and
that's that. This is not a job application, nor is it my resume; it is my life
experience as part of my personal brand.

You may need to do the same thing: a descriptive role is often more
helpful than a formal title. Years in the same corporation or in military
service should be summarized in a role (or two) that is meaningful *to the*

reader.

Now enter the organization's name into the "Company" field, and notice that your organization may already be pre-populated on the pull-down menu because someone else has already set that organization up in LinkedIn *(Figure 4.9 shows this feature).*

Like educational institutions, this is a plus because the user's experience will include a link to the organization for more information, and your profile will sport a color logo.

In this example, the first choice in the menu of possible choices with "Intel" in the title is my beloved Intel Corporation, with the correct logo. All indications are that this is the Intel that I worked for in the 1980s, and if I accept this with a click, it will have a big benefit later in our process. So if you see your organization offered in the drop down menu, I definitely recommend that you accept it.

If your organization's name *wasn't* available as a choice, it means you are the first from that organization to setup a profile on the LinkedIn service. It is a fairly simple process to set up an organization, which you can do after you have finished your own brand work—then you can come back and explicitly select your organization from the drop-down list, in order to gain those benefits.

Skip the **Location,** unless it is helpful for your brand. For example, if you were based in Sri Lanka for 2 years and you consider international business experience to be one of your Assets, then that is part of your personal brand... so include it.

Alternatively, the difference between the Intel locations in Santa Clara, California and Hillsboro, Oregon (in my case) isn't interesting enough to include and it is not part of my brand. We want this to be easy to read and brief as possible, so skip location for each position unless it is truly part of your brand.

Next, you are required to enter the date range for your work in this role. As previously discussed, I advocate entering *only the year* in the date range of your service in each role—leave out the month. Nobody cares. Clutters up the format when reading on a smartphone, and again, brevity is king.

Finally and most importantly, copy from your working document the narrative you wrote for this position and paste it into the **Description** window. You should have already checked for typos and punctuation, but take one more look. If your narrative for this role runs long, consider the use of vertical "white space" to help make it easier to read; it is best if you are so brief that such white space isn't needed.

Also note the **Media** area just below the **Description** window. This is meant to encourage you to upload various media such as video and photos. Ignore these for now also—we'll talk about this in just a moment.

If you're good with this position, then click **Save**.

Congratulations, you have your first entry in your life experience loaded into the LinkedIn service!

Now click on the "+" symbol again, and paste the next entry from your Life Experience in your working document.

Note that you do *not* have to make each position in chronological order—LinkedIn will use the date range of service to display each role in the proper chronological order.

Building On The Foundation

With two layers of your framework in place in the LinkedIn service, you have the core of your brand ready. Now we'll start adding a few more dimensions to the picture. See Fig 4.10 on the next page.

VOLUNTEER EXPERIENCE

LinkedIn allows you to enter multiple positions in the **Volunteer Experience** section, but I strongly recommend you *avoid this* and instead make those entries in the **Experience** section.

I recommend that you place your volunteer work in the context of your paid work, because I assume you acted professionally regardless of whether you were paid or worked for free. And placing your volunteer work in that same context helps the reader "see" you more accurately and more authentically.

I recommend simply leaving the Volunteer Experience blank (it won't be displayed in your profile if nothing is in it).

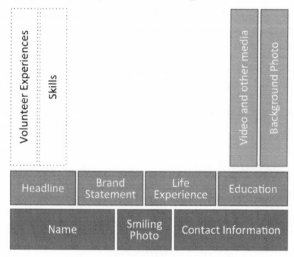

Figure 4.10 Don't put your volunteer experience in the Volunteer Section, and never itemize your skills (I will explain why). Do consider uploading a video and background photo.

SKILLS SECTION

Leave this section blank. We want the viewer's eye to be drawn to your summary first (your Brand Statement) and unfortunately the **Skills** section is distracting.

And it is essentially a laundry list without narratives or evidence, and as a result, the **Skills** section doesn't have much credibility. So why is it offered?

To understand, we have to talk about Faust.

FAUST AND YOUR BRAND

As you review your LinkedIn presence, it is vital to understand the contract you are making with LinkedIn. While you are not surrendering your moral integrity in exchange for power and success (as Faust reputedly did) you *are* entering into a contract.

You do not need a premium account with LinkedIn to host your brand. The entry-level, free account provides everything that you need. (LinkedIn would be delighted to sell you a premium upgrade, which we will discuss later).

However, in exchange for free hosting of your presence on LinkedIn in the entry-level account, they will use the data in your LinkedIn presence to make money from other parties. This is a key component of their business model.

Obviously, I've made peace with the explicit contract I've made with LinkedIn over the past 14 years—they can use, or even resell, my personal data, and in fair exchange, I will take full advantage of their free hosting and access to 467 million people.

The key to my arrangement with LinkedIn is my commitment (to myself) to engage only the features that serve my purpose and to ignore the requests (framed as offers) from LinkedIn that do not.

My purpose is to present my authentic self to the world, efficiently and effectively. What does this mean?

A good example is the request that I specify my expertise in the **Skills** section. Seems like a reasonable offer, eh?

Not so fast. In my experience, a **Skills** section displayed in your profile to others takes up a great deal of real estate on the screen and disrupts the reader's experience of skimming your profile.

I strongly recommend you do not accept the offer. It is not consistent with the purpose of your LinkedIn presence, as we just defined.

So why is it there?

Because these keywords enable database searching, profile matching, a type of data that can be resold and/or used with other parties.

I think it's fair for the LinkedIn service to keep inviting me, but I'm going to keep skipping this. I urge you to make similar decisions, simply evaluate each offer for how it supports the purpose of your brand presence.

BACKGROUND PHOTO

You have probably noticed that in addition to a picture of you, LinkedIn allows you to upload a photo that spreads across the top of your profile (see my LinkedIn Profile for an example). Visual elements are always part of a brand, and you should consider making a thoughtful and unique photo part of your brand.

Open your profile for editing, and when you find a "pen" icon for editing the background photo in the upper right corner. You will be guided through the process of uploading and cropping the image.

VIDEO AND OTHER MEDIA

Videos of a wide variety have become commonplace in social media such as **Twitter, Instagram** and **Facebook**. As the business form of social media, LinkedIn is experiencing this trend as well—and it is un-likely to taper any time soon. On the contrary, you will see more video and even virtual reality in the future.

If you have video that represents you, or communicates an aspect of your brand, then definitely consider including it in your LinkedIn Profile.

You can use video as a status post (more about that in **Part 6**) and you can use it as a "permanent" part of your profile -- either coupled with your Brand Statement or with one or more positions in your Life Experience.

Note the "Upload" and "Link" buttons offered in Figure 4.11 on the next page.

Figure 4.11 Each Experience position and Education role can be augmented with media uploaded or linked.

See Figure 4.12 on the next page for a good example of using video to help buttress a brand statement.

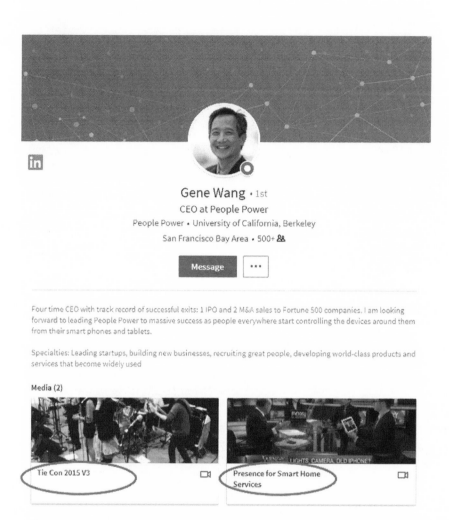

Figure 4.12 Video can be used effectively to improve or even replace the text in your LinkedIn Profile. In this example, it is part of Gene Wang's brand statement.

Gene Wang has chosen to use one clip from an interview on *Fox Business* television about his current startup, **People Power**. In support of Gene's brand, the video provides credibility that the company is attracting national attention (e.g. the *Fox Network*) and also provides a visual experience of one of People Power's products. As a bonus, you get to "meet" Gene by hearing him talk and watching him on the program.

He has also chosen to use another clip providing a glimpse into the playful (and talented) crew, a rock band made up of team members performing at a popular conference in Silicon Valley. I can testify that this is an authentic side of Gene—playful and musical—and thus a good reason to include it in his brand statement.

ACCOMPLISHMENTS

LinkedIn currently offers nine different "accomplishment" sections for inclusion in your profile (the exact number and type of sections fluctuates over time).

As you can see in Figure 4.13 below, these complete the framework of your LinkedIn Profile:

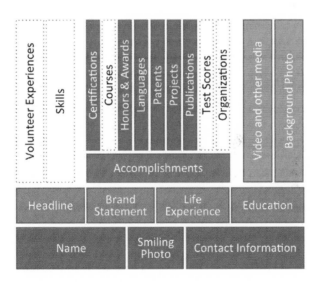

Figure 4.13 To minimize clutter and overall size, careful thought should be given to which Accomplishments are included, if any.

We'll go through each of these nine sections within the Accomplishments block in the following pages, and discuss the appropriateness of each for your specific situation.

CERTIFICATIONS SECTION

Some are tempted to include this section in their profile, and even fill it to the brim with 10 or 20 certifications. After all, certifications often represent a great deal of work. But like keywords in the **Skills** Section and a long list of accomplishments in the **Experience** section, your certifications probably aren't as interesting as your passions. So leave them out, unless they are an essential part of your brand.

There are exceptions, such as our architect with the pilot's license.

For example, if your industry is oceanography and you are passionate about underwater welding, you might want to include that certification as a point of interest, a dimension of your capabilities that is unique in comparison to others in your industry.

Certain certifications prove a mastery in a skill, often requiring more than 10,000 hours of experience, such as a sailor with the "dolphins" indicating *Submariner* qualification, a surgeon achieving board certification after years of residency following medical school, and the *U.S. Coast Guard Unlimited Master Mariner* license (command any ship, of any size). These lifetime accomplishments help the viewer connect the dots about who you are and what you love, so include them.

But don't look for excuses to include your certifications in a laundry list. For example, as a firefighter/EMT and rescuer for decades, I have many professional certifications relevant to that work—but I don't list all of them in my LinkedIn Profile because it could be distracting as I attempt to balance the three dimensions of my brand between executive coach, bicycle guide, and firefighter/EMT.

Professions that require detailed and specific certifications, such as medicine, firefighting, law enforcement and military service will already have a convention for listing (and verifying) these certifications, and it won't be on the LinkedIn service. On LinkedIn, they will want to summarize the certifications in a way that illuminates their personal brand.

COURSES SECTION

It is difficult to imagine a personal brand that would highlight an individual course, since any such experience in academia would be better served in the context of the **Education** Section. And a course that led to a certain certification would be best served in the **Certifications** Section discussed previously.

Don't use this section.

HONORS & AWARDS SECTION

An exhaustive list of every award and honor usually isn't appropriate. It would communicate a certain, um, emphasis on *accomplishment.* Consistent with the rest of your brand, you want to illuminate your Assets, not boast of your accomplishments.

That said, certain honors would be a part of an authentic profile. How to decide whether to include your award for your 9th grade spelling bee performance?

A good rule of thumb is to include the honor if you think your colleagues would view it as meaningful; don't include it only if your parents and relatives would be proud. But don't hide what makes you great.

LANGUAGES SECTION

By all means, list your languages and specify your proficiency. This is definitely part of your brand.

PATENTS SECTION

If you have patents, include them. But leave out the description and provide only the number, date, and an abbreviated title *(anyone familiar with patents knows how to find yours online, given the number).*

If you have more than five, as some of my high technology clients do, then consider listing just 5–8 in this way, and then offer a text block in Activities that says "…and 23 more patents in related technologies, list available separately."

Unlike a CV, we're not making a formal accounting of all accomplishments… we're attempting to portray a sense of the individual. In fact, "List of patents available separately" says accomplishment *very clearly*. You've made your point, and it is part of your brand. Don't exhaust the reader with a laundry list.

PROJECTS SECTION

I *don't* recommend you list every project that you've worked on in your career, or even some of them—most should leave this section blank.

However, if your accomplishments are best illuminated by projects you've done, then use this section to provide a sense of those accomplishments.

For example, if you are an artist with many installations over the years, this may be a more tidy and efficient way to list your exhibitions than the **Publications** section or the **Experience** section. Musicians, actors, and directors may also find this more suitable for listing their work.

Writers should generally use the **Publications** section, but for certain circumstances the **Projects** section may be more appropriate.

The rest of us should leave it blank.

PUBLICATIONS SECTION

Treat this in the same way as the **Patents** section—summarize to minimize clutter, and provide enough information that a reader can click through to actually read the publication.

TEST SCORES

It is hard to imagine a score on any specific test that would rise to the level of being a key aspect of a personal brand. A particular achievement worthy of emphasis should be placed in the context of the academic experience—in the **Education** Section.

All of us should leave this section blank.

ORGANIZATIONS

This is a "general purpose" section, And you won't need it because you have captured all of the relevant organizations in your Life Experience.

Most of us should leave this section blank.

ACTIVITIES SECTION

This is another "general purpose" section, which you may want to use in the same way that artists would use the **Projects** section—any collection of accomplishments that doesn't fit cleanly into any of the other sections.

For example, say you sailed around the world single-handed, or you hiked the length of the Pacific Crest Trail, or you were asked to contribute prose for a Dr. Seuss book on science for children (a real example for a friend of mine). The kind of thing that would be revealed in a good, deep interview... but wouldn't be on a resume. If it didn't fit easily into the **Experience** section, then you might place it here.

Most of us will leave it blank.

RECOMMENDATIONS SECTION

The final section of your framework are the **Recommendations** you receive from (and provide to) others. We will discuss this in detail in **Part 6.** Leave this blank, for now.

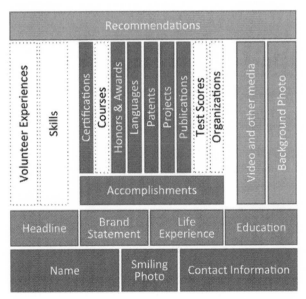

Figure 4.14 Recommendations are the capstone of your framework.

PART 5:
Launching LinkedIn

A ship in harbor is safe, but that is not what ships are built for.

~John A. Shedd

IT IS NEARLY TIME TO launch your brand on the LinkedIn service, now that you've uploaded your hard work. But not so fast, we need to do a few last things before you show your brand to the world.

Review of Your Profile

Take one last pass through all of the sections of your profile. You're looking for typos, mistakes, and frankly, wordiness. Don't be afraid to edit and trim for brevity.

When you do this, be sure to carefully check your finished work by using **View Profile** so that you see what visitors will actually see. Then ask a friend or colleague to do the same.

Remember to also grab your phone and view your profile through the limited space of that device.

Current Experience

Recently, the LinkedIn service disabled the ability for you to change the order in which each section of your profile was presented to a viewer. I used to recommend utilizing this feature to fine-tune the presentation of your profile, for the benefit of your brand. While this is no longer available, there is a relatively subtle ordering feature that may apply to you.

This is an issue if you have two (or more) "current positions" in your **Experience** section—say a volunteer role and a paid role in two different organizations. You will want to specify which role is *shown first*. I recommend the paid role first.

Figure 5.1 below shows how to do this, which is to hover your mouse in the vicinity of the "pen" icon for edit, and notice the "menu stack" icon *(aka "hamburger bun")* becomes visible. Click on this, and move the current role to the ordered position you want.

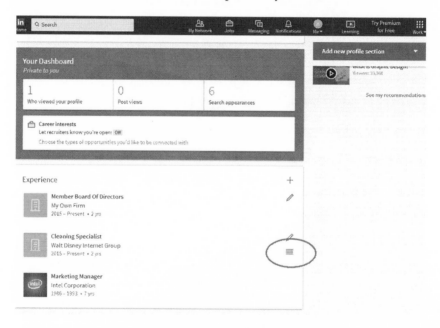

Figure 5.1 Hover over the "menu stack" to change the order.

Going Live

Now that you've wrapped up these last details, you're ready to go live.

When you are confident that the errors and typos have been caught and that your brand is ready to be seen, then revisit where you turned OFF updates to your network, and turn that ON.

Then make one change, anywhere in your profile. I like to upload my photograph (even though I already have one loaded), since that will trigger a message out to my network… "David has a new profile photograph."

An even *better* choice is to use load your most recent "job" in the **Experience** section last, after you've turned Network Updates on. Almost everyone is intrigued when they hear you have a new job, and they will click through to check it out.

Either of these actions will alert your network to your existence, and word will spread.

Well done!

PART 6:
Care and Feeding Of Your Brand

*The road to success is always under
construction.*

~Arnold Palmer

ALMOST EVERYTHING PROVIDED IN THIS book so far either develops or hones your brand. The work you have done to present your brand in your LinkedIn profile also establishes your credibility as a professional in your field with a grasp of a modern tool with global reach.

But.

That's not enough. You can't just leave it there.

In the same way that you cannot build a website for your business and then ignore it, or set up an email address but not check it for incoming email. You need to keep your brand on the LinkedIn service alive and well.

First we'll talk about several key responsibilities for maintaining an effective brand presence, not just a static profile.

Then we'll address the issue of credibility. You could have the most thoughtful, effective and articulate LinkedIn Profile on the Internet, but if you don't have a number of connections and recommendations, you will lack credibility. We'll address each of those issues in turn.

Finally, we'll touch on the issue of remaining active on LinkedIn, which is not strictly a requirement for your brand—but is a good idea if you're interesting in getting a different job, building a new career, establishing a business, accessing a potential new customer, or otherwise promoting a cause (including yourself).

Accuracy

It should be obvious, but you'll need to keep your life experience up to date. Some of us have avoided keeping our paper resume up to date, particularly when we're enjoying our work and have no interest in looking for a new job.

But that mindset doesn't make sense with your brand.

Your brand will continue to evolve, as you move through your career (or your post-retirement). You will meet more people, work on different projects, learn new skills, and be intrigued by different topics and industries.

As you may recall from **Part 1**, your brand is how you become more efficient in your relationships with people—vendors, customers, employees, employers, volunteer organizations and colleagues. If your brand doesn't keep up with your reality, then you erode the efficiency that you originally sought.

At a minimum, your contact information needs to be kept up to date. This may appear simple (how long have you had that phone number?) but this is deceptive. Part of your "contact information" is the context by which the people in your network know you—they need to know where you currently work (whether volunteer or paid).

So keeping your profile up to date with your constantly evolving brand means examining all of the sections of your LinkedIn Profile as you created them in the exerecises of this book.

Schedule

My recommendation is to set an event in your calendar **every 90 days** (four times a year) to update your **Experience** section for what you've done most recently. Return to the method described in this book for drafting a narrative of any new experience, and remember to emphasize how it relates to your Assets (rather than what you accomplished).

I am confident that in your life you will see new opportunities (and take some of them). For many of us, we have a set of passions that are constant for years (perhaps decades?) but others that may shift during the course of the year. Your vacation, for example, may awake a long-dormant passion for painting, photography, travel, or sailing. A new project at work may remind you that you've always enjoyed teaching and mentoring.

In the midst of vacation or the intensity of a job assignment, you may not be thinking about your brand and how it may be evolving. The quarterly schedule of pausing to evaluate your brand is a good way for noticing the change, the addition to your life experience.

And I recommend that **once a year**, you take a significant pause to review your list of Assets. For most of us, our Assets will not change throughout the year.

But you might be surprised by new Assets that emerge over time. As you realize these Assets, work them into your life experience following the method you learned in **Part 3**. Yes, it's okay if your profile gets a bit longer each time.

Remember the overall concept: you are connecting the dots for your reader so they can get to know the authentic you at a glance, without interviewing you.

Number Of Connections

You've gone to some effort to ensure that your profile is professional, with an appropriate photo and no typos or errors. Your effective use of the LinkedIn service and your thoughtful presentation of your unique brand both establish your professional credibility. Another source of credibility for your brand is the *number of connections* to your profile.

There is no rigid rule, but in my experience if you have fewer than 250–300 connections, then many viewers will not regard you as a credible user of modern business tools.

It doesn't mean you're not successful, capable, or awesome. It just means that you look like the kind of person who just heard about cell phones and websites…and is considering getting one someday.

As I've said previously, for professionals in most industries there is no negative judgment for being a "late adopter" of technology (obviously, this can erode your credibility in a high technology industry). In fact, for some, being a late adopter is a sign of mature and careful judgment.

But at the same time, if you are a late adopter there is no way to avoid leaving the impression that you're slow to use technology tools, and thus you're not putting your best foot forward professionally.

As a general rule of thumb, if your profile shows 500+ connections, then viewers know that you're using the LinkedIn tool… and that you also know a reasonable number of people. From their selfish perspective, your value (to them) is increased. Remember, success in any field is about relationships, and you obviously have them.

BUILD A BASE

So how do you get enough connections to be credible, if you're starting from zero. Or if you haven't been active for the past couple of years, say because you're returning to the workforce after raising a family?

Perhaps you're ready to settle down into some serious volunteering after retiring, and feeling like you don't know many people outside of your previous career?

Don't be intimidated—this is straightforward.

START WITH WHO YOU KNOW

The first step in building your base is deceptively simple: *only connect with people you already know.*

Despite the original thesis of LinkedIn, to provide a way of connecting with strangers via shared connections, it still isn't very effective or natural. And you probably don't need it.

Even if you are returning to the workforce after a long time away, you already know hundreds of people: neighbors, friends of the family, distant family, former colleagues, teachers, and students. You have probably been a part of a club or two, a church, a community—while you may think of that as a group, it is made up of individuals who you know by name. Even if you only know each other by first name, you know them.

And of all the people you know, at least *one out of every two* are already on LinkedIn, which had 133 million members in the U.S. (as of Spring 2017), which is 65% of the U.S. population (2016 adults 18–65). Obviously this is a statistical point of view, given that LinkedIn is more likely a venue for college-educated, white collar people than tradespeople and blue collar, so the ratio in your specific network may be different. For many of us, it will be much higher. The point is, you have a *roughly 50% chance of finding every person you know* by name on LinkedIn.

LinkedIn also provides a nifty tool that will import your contacts from your **Outlook, Gmail, Hotmail,** or **Yahoo** address book. This tool will quickly provide a visual confirmation of which of your contacts are already on the LinkedIn service. This is a fine way to get an initial list of potential connections—from the people you already know.

Or you can dedicate an hour or two each day for a week or so, typing in the names of people you know into the **Search** box on the LinkedIn service.

If you can't remember their full name, consider the **Advanced Search** window, which allows you to narrow by geography, industry, and company name.

For instance, this gives you a way to find the name of that fellow you like at church, but can only remember his first name and that he used to work for the Acme company. His photo on his profile will confirm your successful search.

Another way that easily finds people you already know is to click on the profile of a colleague that you know well, and use the LinkedIn feature for seeing her connections. You will likely know people she is connected to, that you know too.

Click on their profiles, and check out what they've been doing (and how active they are on LinkedIn and how many connections they have on LinkedIn). You may be surprised to find some of your closest friends on LinkedIn using this technique.

I don't recommend sitting down to obsessively chase down every person you know, for hours at a time. Make it a practice, and keep it to an hour (or less) on a regular basis, once a day or once a week until you get to 500. How does a mouse eat an elephant?

MAKING THE CONNECTION

First, be sure you are looking at the *actual full profile* of the individual. If you're looking at a list of contacts, *do not* click on **Connect** for any of these contacts (more about this in a moment). Instead, click on their profile picture or their name, and get all the way to their full profile *before you do anything else.*

Once you are looking at the profile page, notice there is a button under their picture/name/headline. Click on this highlighted button **Connect** as you can see in the example of Figure 6.1 below, where I want to connect with Dave Noda.

Note that the screen shown in Figure 6.1 is for a free, basic account on the LinkedIn service. Premium LinkedIn accounts may show other buttons offering services such as **InMail, Follow** and other options.

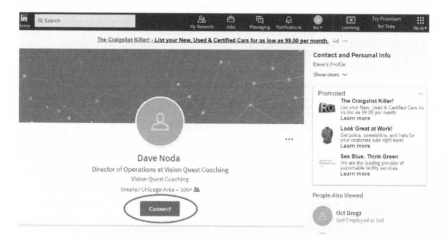

Figure 6.1 Use the Connect option to start the process of connecting with Dave Noda.

After you click the **Connect**, you will be presented with a dialog box shown in Figure 6.2, inviting you to customize the invitation to connect.

Always do this. This is an essential part of making a good connection, so click on the **Add a note** button.

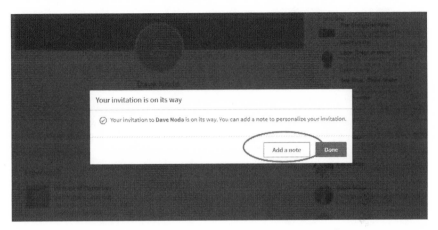

Figure 6.2 Your invite has not actually been sent yet, because you can Add A Note. Always do this.

You can write nearly anything in your note to this contact, but I like to use their first name again and put something legitimately unique in the note. Anything to help communicate that I am not spam and not an automatic request, but a thoughtful request to connect.

The procedure for inviting a connection and demonstrating that you have previous contact is in place for two reasons.

It makes the obvious spam attempts a tiny bit more difficult, but most of all it tells the recipient why they know you and what the context is for your relationship (which may be nascent).

As you may have already experienced if you already have a LinkedIn account, you will receive requests for connections from complete strangers (more about that in a moment). They seem to always use the default, automatic request note. When I receive one of these, my assumption is that the request *is spam*. And so I ignore it.

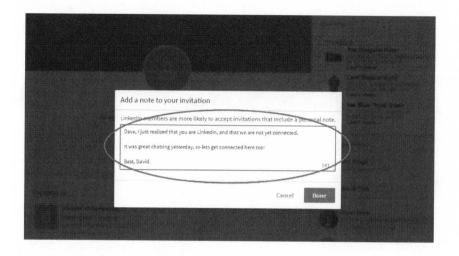

Figure 6.3 When I add my note, I like to use my friend's name again, and to put the request in context, and sign it with my name too. So the other person knows it is not spam.

CAUTION: AVOID THE AUTOMATIC CONNECT

A well-intended feature of LinkedIn can trip you up.

After you make a connection request following the procedure just described, you will be presented with an array of faces and names titled "People you may know."

And indeed, you may know some of them. I see familiar names every time. This is a good thing.

You will also be presented with a version of this screen if you click on **My Network** in the ribbon navigation strip across the top of your window.

When you see this, I want you to be *careful*. There is a right way and a wrong way to take advantage of this helpful feature.

While he hasn't been top of mind, when I clicked on this to grab this screen, I saw the smiling face of Hooks Johnson. I haven't talked to him in years, but he is a talented guy that I worked with back in the day. I'd like to reconnect with him.

You might reasonably assume the next thing to do is click the Connect button directly under his face and name (see Figure 6.4).

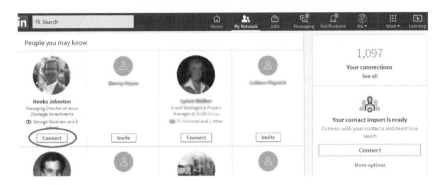

Figure 6.4 Do not click Connect in the gallery of people you may know, there is a better way. (The other faces in this view have been deliberately blurred to protect their identity)

Do *not* click on **Connect**.

Designed for speed apparently, clicking on this launches an "automatic" invite to the individual without any further effort on your part—which arrives looking like spam. Do not do this!

Instead click on the name of the individual or photo of the individual.

As previously described, when you click on their name instead, you will be delivered to their *full profile*. Great, now you can catch up on what he's doing and where he's been since you last interacted. A good practice.

And then you follow the procedure just described for making a personal connection, adding a personal note providing context and not-spam evidence.

There is another gotcha in this interface: note that some of the blue buttons say **Invite** instead of **Connect**. This is actually *worse* than the automatic connection request.

Connect means they are already on LinkedIn but not connected to you; **Invite** means they aren't even on LinkedIn yet… and the automatic email sent will *invite them to join* LinkedIn, and identify you as the person who suggested that they join the service. While I appreciate LinkedIn's effort to expand their service, this kind of unsolicited commercial request isn't going to end well. It will probably be experienced as literal spam, from you. *Never click on **Invite**.*

ACCEPTING INVITATIONS

As you improve your LinkedIn presence, you will surely receive requests for connections from others. This is a good thing, but don't accept any of them blindly.

Follow this procedure every single time: click on the profile, and verify that you actually know the person. *Then* accept the invitation.

Generally speaking, if you do not know the person *do not accept the invitation.* It is as simple as that (we'll talk about exceptions to this guideline in just a moment).

If you accept an invitation that you later regret, it is easy (and discreet) to sever the connection. Simply go to their profile and hover your cursor on the blue action box beneath their name and adjacent to their profile picture. The drop down menu will offer several options, such as **View Recent Activity** and **Share Profile**. The last option is **Remove Connection**.

There are exceptions to avoiding strangers. In certain situations, you may find yourself wanting to know and even connect with strangers. One of my clients sells to people who ride bicycles, so when she receives a connect request from a complete stranger, a quick check of the profile tells her what she needs to know. If she can verify their reputation and their interest in bicycles (via a thoughtful and deliberate profile), then she may accept the invitation from a stranger.

If you are in the business of sales, requests for connection may not be spam—it may be a symptom that your marketing is working. So click on that profile and check them out. If you see evidence that they could be a customer, then accept the invite. Note that this is another argument for presenting an authentic brand, including your personal interests, in your LinkedIn Profile.

If you have reviewed the profile and you're still not sure, consider sending the requesting individual a message...asking for clarification.

By the way, sending messages via the LinkedIn **InMail** system doesn't expose your personal email address, and for some recipients it is the only way to get them a message (because their email address isn't easily accessible). This is a service only available to premium customers. Expect a delay for responses to InMail messages, as the InMail inbox isn't checked constantly by recipients the way they check their regular email.

ANOTHER CAUTION: AVOID REACHING OUT FROM YOUR PHONE

As of this writing, the **Connect** button when used on the iPhone or iPad will not offer the manual, customized message—it will simply launch an automatic invite with a generic message.

It does not appear to be possible to send a personalized request for connection on LinkedIn from a mobile device at the current time, so my advice is *not to do it*. Wait until you're on a computer with a full-featured browser. Otherwise your invite may be seen as spam.

MOMENTUM

How many people should you attempt to make connection with on LinkedIn? As previously stated, a minimum of 250 is a good target— but 500 is even better.

Why? As you get above 500 connections, the display to others on your profile will show "500+" rather than the exact number of your connections. When you get to 500, the viewer can't tell if you have 501 or 1,000 connections. Simply get to this threshold.

Pro tip: if you want to know how many you have, simply click on **My Network** in the top navigation ribbon, and you will see your total connections in the upper left of the screen.

As you reach out to people you already know, you will likely see an increasing rate of requests from others. This is because LinkedIn is updating your network with the news that you have new connections, and some people will see this… and it will remind them that they know you, and that they should stay in touch. This often has a kind of snowball effect: picking up speed and more contacts as it "rolls down hill." So start building that base now.

I often suggest to clients to set aside 10–20 minutes each week to process the outstanding invitations coming in from others, and to use the LinkedIn tool to search for people you may know.

While you don't want to let the incoming requests distract you from your regular work, you do need to regularly "water your garden."

The dedication of that small amount of time each week will likely serve you very well in increasing the size of your network. The mouse eats the elephant.

FOLLOWING

For public figures of influence, there could be thousands of requests for connection. If you are one of these, or if you know one of these, you will see a practice of careful acceptance. Public figures will typically use a LinkedIn option that requires any individual requesting connection specify the email address of the recipient (theirs), as a hurdle that verifies they already know them.

The rest of us have an option: you can choose to **Follow** these individuals. Note the **Follow** option, next to the **Connect** option. Note that in a subtle way, your choice of individuals to follow becomes part of your brand, because this information is revealed in the full view of your LinkedIn Profile.

A PRACTICE OF INCLUSION

One simple rule you may consider as you go forward in your business, in your career, or especially in retirement: add each person you meet to your network. In other words, when you meet someone in your work, at a party, or in nearly any context, make it a practice to jot down their name (or use that old-school technique, accept one of their business cards).

When you get home (or during your weekly 10-20 minute Linke-dIn garden-watering) use the search function in the LinkedIn service, and send them a personal invitation, using the procedure described here.

Once you're connected, you have a way of reaching them again. You don't need to enter them in your contact database, if you have one. And your network is a bit larger.

I try to follow this practice, and I'm often amazed at the shared contacts and interconnected relationships that emerge when I enter a new "stranger" into my LinkedIn network.

I think of it as inclusion, but I'm also lightening my load for keeping track of people and their email addresses.

Recommendations

Just as with a minimum number of connections, for credibility with viewers that have experience with LinkedIn, your profile should feature several references by colleagues. I recommend at least 6, and no more than 20.

LinkedIn calls these **Recommendations**, which are different than **Endorsements**. I'm not a fan of **Endorsements** (as currently imple-mented by LinkedIn) but **Recommendations** can be an effective dimension of your brand.

The key to effective **Recommendations** that support your brand is to ask for them deliberately and mindfully. Ensure that they are authen-tic, and see if each Recommendation can speak to one or more of your specific Assets.

In general, one or two recommendations for each of your significant life experiences is ideal, as long as you don't overwhelm your viewer (thus the suggested limit of 20).

This isn't hard. As with all "asks", it goes best in person, second-best by phone, and only by last resort, via email.

Here's the method that I have seen work well:

1. Return to your **Experience** section, and for each job/experience, consider one person who knows you well, who would likely

agree to comment on an Asset (or two) that you demonstrated in that role. Pencil in their name, and the Asset. If you have five entries in **Experience,** that's 5–10 names. If you have 10 entries, that's 10–20 names. If you have more than 10 entries, I would plan on no more than one person per role, and perhaps skip some of the roles. You do not want to create an overwhelming amount of text in the **Recommendation** section.

2. Put the list in priority, based on the credibility (and brand) of each potential recommender. You can rule out anyone who isn't active on LinkedIn, or has a sparse LinkedIn profile. That will defeat the purpose of the recomendation when a viewer clicks through to learn more about them.

3. Get on the phone (or book lunch or coffee) with each. Don't overdo it. Start out with just the first five on your list.

4. When you meet with them, either in person or by phone, make the ask. Explain that you've just finished updating your Linke-dIn Profile to serve as a personal brand, and that you'd like their help *(feel free to tell them about the method in this book)*. In my experience, this is a topic of interest... and most potential rec-ommenders will take it as a sign that you're serious about this, and they'll correspondingly do their best. Reassure them you will send a reminder email.

5. Send the follow-up email promptly, that day if at all possible. Perhaps compose it in advance, so there is no reason for delay. The email should be short and to the point. Provide a link to your (custom) LinkedIn URL and a polite request that they submit a recommendation for you, perhaps highlighting the Asset you identified.

The LinkedIn system will manage their submission and send it to you for your approval before posting it in your profile—so don't fret about your recommender writing something inappropriate by accident. You get a chance to review and approve, and I urge you to suggest edits if you think it will improve the recommendation.

You can even leave a recommendation inactive (or make it inactive) utilizing the **Show** slider switch in each recommendation (slide it to off).

Pause when you've done five of these, and consider the effect these have had on your brand. You may not need any more, but if you decide you need more, then repeat the process with the next five on your list.

I often advise my clients that provide services to solicit a written recommendation from a client or customer at the conclusion of a significant project, or period of work. In the afterglow of a successful engagement the details will still be relevant, and participants most conducive to a review. And perhaps you (and your recommender) will not be caught up yet in the next assignment. Asking for a review via the LinkedIn recommendation process is a great way to streamline this request, for both parties.

Remember to include the **Recommendations** Section in your every-90-day review of your brand and LinkedIn profile.

Out of Sight, Out of Mind

We've addressed the two most significant factors for the credibility of your brand on the LinkedIn service: number of connections and recommendations. There is a third factor, which can improve credibility, and also aid you if you are promoting a cause (including if you yourself are the cause, such as in a job search).

If you remain active on LinkedIn, then part of your network will "see" your activity. With that visibility, your profile is more likely to be viewed. In turn, you are more likely to be remembered when the viewer encounters an opportunity suitable for you.

In other words, out of sight, out of mind.

This is not relevant to everyone reading this book. It *is* relevant if you're looking for a job, always on the hunt for great opportunities (as Kevin Bacon is, hoping the telephone will ring). It *is* relevant if you're looking for great vendors, partners, customers, and employees.

To be seen is to be remembered, and being remembered for a specific opportunity is half the battle in sales. Our world is so busy, so filled with stimulating inputs that it is difficult to remember that so-and-so would be perfect for the project, the sale, the gig, or the job.

If you want to be seen on the LinkedIn service, there are three ways I recommend:

- "Like" or comment on someone else's status post
- Post your own status post (usually an article you think relevant)
- Post about your latest blog entry

If you already have a blog, you absolutely should post a tempting snippet from each blog entry on your LinkedIn status window, with a link to the blog.

A more realistic and efficient way to handle this process is to utilize a plug-in from within the platform for your blog posts *(for example, WordPress)* to automatically publish your blog posts authored there, on your LinkedIn presence.

Sharing your blog posts on LinkedIn has multiple advantages for your brand: it increases SEO (search engine optimization), it helps communicate your brand and brand messages via a different medium than your profile, and it could positively impact the number of connections and/or followers on LinkedIn.

There is virtually no downside, unless your posts are unprofessional or riddled with errors. You wouldn't do that, would you?

PART 7:
Results

We can easily forgive a child who is afraid of the dark; the real tragedy of life is when men are afraid of the light.

~Plato

SOME CLIENTS WONDER IF ALL the work to create a personal brand is really worth it. Some are even brave enough to admit it out loud, so you are not alone if you're questioning this too. After all, you probably already have hobbies, friends, and family... and a job.

A case can be made that you really don't have a choice, that it is essentially impossible to participate in society and not be visible online, in some way.

I know a handful of people in the age range of 18 to 65 who are not online, but they have become a very rare breed. Those resisting the pull of the Internet represent less than 1% of all the people I know, and I suspect your statistic is similar.

A more common condition is that individuals are online, but have not prepared a thoughtful presentation of themselves. Let alone considered how they convey their personal brand, or even fail to consider themselves worthy of "a brand."

People like this have a few photos posted on Facebook or Instagram, perhaps use twitter to read (and sometimes post) about news and famous personalities, and perhaps they've described a bare minimum of work history in their LinkedIn Profile. What is their fate in this age of social media?

In my experience, they will miss opportunities. And it is the nature of missed opportunities that they'll rarely be made aware of the thing that didn't happen. How could they?

But I assure you, miss opportunities they will. An example: one of the fascinating dimensions of social media is the ability for others to find you. Old friends, colleagues, even family can stumble across you in social media, a kind of serendipity if the timing is right. You've heard these stories, or even lived them yourself. Some stories are pretty amazing, and have even led to marriage.

The business and professional equivalent of this kind of serendipity is the job possibility never discussed, the nonprofit board position never offered, and the sale never made.

Another implication of not participating in social media for professional reasons is that you limit the size of your community. The circle of people who can support and help you will be limited to the people you meet in person. This is obviously a finite number of people.

But our only motivation shouldn't be *fear of missing out*. There are amazing opportunities, too.

Opportunities

Most of my clients are executives and entrepreneurs, well along in their careers. Most have developed relatively large networks of 500 to 2,500 contacts. Unlike those seeking their first real job, my clients tend to know a lot of people, and they're well known themselves.

By taking the step to define their unique brand, they really take *ownership* of their presence, and they inevitably make their presence more focused.

They have chosen what they really want to do, and they have taken the effort to prove (through their **Experience** section) that they have done it before, and can do it again.

Even with the benefit of relatively large personal networks, they have new opportunities. It's simple, really—prior to defining their brand, they have not been *specific* and *deliberate* about what they really want. Without that visible brand, how could the members of their network possibly know what they want?

By using the LinkedIn service to host their thoughtful, considered brand, they are viewed more crisply and effectively *every time* a member of their network sees their LinkedIn profile. *Repitition* of a brand is a well-known component of effective branding.

As a result, the very essence of business, the relationship, is more efficient and more focused. They have figuratively greased the gears of their profession.

You've already read in this book about the talented architect who works in the career he *loves* doing aviation architecture. Allow me to share a few more:

I have a client who accepted a seat on a board of directors of a startup company, and then refined his brand to emphasize board service in the context of his experience. Within a single year he had acquired several more board member positions.

Another client had a stellar record in design and software user interface work, and was ready to transform her long-time passion for virtual reality into paying work. She now works primarily in virtual reality.

A first-time startup founder sought my help, and we put his diverse background (not directly related to technology) in the context of the needs of the startup for definitive leadership. His refined personal brand was a factor in landing initial financing, and the company is now on its way. It isn't necessarily the LinkedIn Profile that made it happen, but the individual really *owns* and lives their personal brand.

The examples go on. Each with different factors, but all with a common thread: specific Assets are illuminated, credibility is improved, and the uniqueness of the individual is illuminated clearly and crisply. Every time, the passion of the individual is more accessible.

Your brand is going to stand out, if for no other reason than you have carefully and deliberately created it for viewing by your colleagues and future contacts.

Stop hiding what makes you great, and shine a light on what you really want to do.

Last Word

As you followed the methodology in this book, you might also have noticed that you've become more aware, more sensitive to like-minded souls. You now realize which people in *your* network have been careful and thoughtful about their personal brand. You now notice a good LinkedIn Profile, with the right picture.

As a result, you now know what they want, how they present themselves to the world, and you probably have a good idea about where they're headed. Keep an eye on them. If they're not already successful, they will be soon.

And those are relationships to foster. Which will be easier for you now, because they'll see you in the same light.

FOR MORE

If you'd like free worksheets that facilitate the exercises described in this book, visit http://FlashingRedLight.com/Books.

I maintain a *Hall of Fame* of noteworthy personal brands hosted as LinkedIn Profiles. These may serve as examples for you as you do your own work, and also recognizes excellent work. This too can be seen at http://FlashingRedLight.com/Books.

ACKNOWLEDGEMENTS

I AM GRATEFUL TO ALL who helped make this happen. Especially the first reviewer of everything I write, my partner and wife Jen Billstrom. I literally couldn't do this without her, and would not have even started this (let alone finished it) except that she insisted upon it.

I want to thank Sharon Purvis and Beth Lohman for editing that helped transform ideas into words that do the job; Karrie Ross for her initial design of the interior book and Leandra Ganko for her usual magician work bridging digital design and technology; and Diane Frisbee for her beautiful cover. Bethany Donovan was invaluable wrestling files, formats, design, and software. I am lucky to have such a professional crew supporting me in this work. Only later did I notice that they are all women.

Compassionate feedback and encouragement from readers of early drafts was essential. Without the early and steady support of Sally, Sean, Dianne, Shannon, Jerry, Barak, and others this would not have come to be. You helped more than you can know.

I have long said that I have learned more from my failures than my successes, particularly when aided by my hubris. And it is also true that I have learned from many others along the way, even though I didn't always realize it, let alone acknowledge it at the time.

Writing a book about presenting yourself as authentically as possible to your professional and personal network made a profound impact on me; reawakening me and reminding me of the difference so many friends and colleagues have made in my life.

Relating the stories in this book required a walk down memory lane, and each story reminded me of another. So many emerged that they couldn't all be included. And each story reminded me of the gratitude that is due to those that I've met along the way, and helped me.

And so overdue thanks is due to many.

This includes: the late David Baty, Barak Berkowitz, Bob Boyd, Laurel Callan, Reuven Carlyle, David Chamberlain, Debi Coleman, Brad Creesy, Jorge Del Calvo, Stan Curtis, Bob Feldman, Manny Friedman, Lisa Gansky, Les Gasser, Michel Gien, Gary Glisson, Mark Goodman, the late Joff Hanauer, Nick Hanauer, Ed Hardy, Steve Kirsch, Reed Koch, Jack Lazar, Ernie Lesley, Dan Lynch, Craig Mc-Clure, Scott McKenzie, Tony McPeak, David McShea, Rich Miller, Mojy Mirashrafi, Noel Monin, Chris Moore, Don Murray, Jim Neuhauser, Will Neuhauser, Mark Olson, Gerry O'Scannlain, Larry Pierson, the late Ginny Rattner, Justin Rattner, Rich Rosen, Graham Ross, Brien Sesby, Scott Shull, Steve Sterba, Elliot Swan, Louis Sweeny, Richard Tait, John Teeter, Allison Tilley, Sam Welsh, Gene Wang, Bob Woodell, and Gerry Zyfers. And keep in mind, that's the short list.

Any teacher knows that whatever experience or even gifts they bring to their students, in the end it is the students that instruct the teacher. It has always been this way, and it is even more so in my coaching practice.

And for that I am profoundly grateful. It is an honor to be trusted by my clients, to hear their fears (and joys), and help them make the most of it. I *always* learn from their hard work.

A few of the many clients who helped and supported me with this work (or assisted quite inadvertently, with a great deal of innocence) would include Neal Andrews, Yoram Bernet, Pete Candler, Steve Cooper, Sean Cunningham, John Daly, Adam Farish, Susanne Hackett, Nadja Haldimann, Cory Harris, Randy Hulett, Jeff Lin, Jeremy Mahon, Eric Morley, Sean Murray, Lindley Myers, Tatum Nolan, Zander Nosler, Peter Polson, Jerry Pope, Chris Preston, Mike Reich, Courtney Smith, Marty Springer, Lisa Tabb, and Terry von Thaden.

I can't even begin to list the entrepreneurs I've encountered in my life as both a fellow entrepreneur and as a venture capitalist. I know for sure I've forgotten many of your names because I'm terrible at that kind of recall, but know that I haven't forgotten your lessons.

Thank you all.

ABOUT THE AUTHOR

DAVID BILLSTROM IS A COACH to entrepreneurs and executives, following a career that included serving as a venture capitalist, board member and advisor, entrepreneur, Intel manager, and Disney vice president.

He has a life-long fascination with what motivates people, fueled by his adventures in launching products, raising money, investing in start-ups, recruiting talent, and participating in more than 700 board meetings.

He also leads a parallel life adventuring in the outdoors, rescuing people in need, and driving a fire engine. He lives far from Silicon Valley in a North Carolina paradise with his wife, dog, and many bicycles.

FUN FACTS

THE IDEA THAT YOU CAN'T unmeet someone as been part of my counsel to clients for years now, so I was delighted to find that bestselling author Jodi Lynn Anderson used the concept in in her book *Tiger Lily.*

The quote from rocker Patti Smith is from a video that captured her speaking at the *Louisiana Literature Festival,* and reflects the advice originally given to her by the writer William S. Burroughs, with regard to her own ambition.

Kevin Bacon gets two mentions in this work, both for the *Bacon Number,* but also for his famously pragmatic work ethic as captured in his statement about waiting for the phone to ring. Indeed.

Blaise Pascal, the French mathematician and philosopher, didn't actually say "I would have written you a shorter letter, but I didn't have time"— he wrote *Je n'ai fait celle-ci plus longue que parce que je n'ai pas eu le loisir de la faire plus courte.* Translated from French, literally "I made this letter very long only because I have not had the leisure to make it shorter." The idea, obviously, is the same. And no, neither Mark Twain nor T.S. Eliot were the originator of the quote. as is often said – it was Pascal. V*ive la France!*

We lost Prince as I worked on an draft of this book, and it seemed only fitting to include his advice about "building" art – appropriate for such a prolific creator, not to speak of his incredible success in creating and maintaining his own personal brand. RIP.

89404174R00095

Made in the USA
Columbia, SC
14 February 2018